NICK MOSELEY

Nick Moseley was born in Trinidad in 1962, the son of a clergyman, and educated at Bristol Grammar School and Royal Holloway, University of London. He worked as an actor in the 1980s before entering the teaching profession in 1990. Nick was Head of Drama, first at a South London comprehensive school and subsequently in a large College of Further Education. In 1997 he became Course Director of the BA (Hons) Acting programme at Italia Conti, where he began to develop his theories and actor-training methodologies. Nick is also a director of the Conference of Drama Schools. In his spare time he restores period homes. He has two children and lives in West London.

ACTING AND REACTING

Tools for the Modern Actor

Nick Moseley

A Theatre Arts Book

Routledge
Taylor & Francis Group

NEW YORK AND LONDON

NICK HERN BOOKS

London

www.nickhernbooks.co.uk

Acting and Reacting:
Tools for the Modern Actor

First published in Great Britain in 2005
as a paperback original by Nick Hern Books Limited,
14 Larden Road, London W3 7ST

First published in the US and Canada in 2006 by
Routledge, 270 Madison Avenue, New York, NY 10016-0602,
by arrangement with Nick Hern Books.
Routledge is an imprint of the Taylor and Francis Group

Cover designed by Peter Bennett

Typeset by Country Setting, Kingsdown, Kent CT14 8ES
Printed and bound in Great Britain
by Cromwell Press, Trowbridge

A CIP catalogue record for this book is available
from the British Library

ISBN-13   978 1 85459 803 5 (UK)
ISBN-10   1 85459 803 1 (UK)

Cataloguing-in-Publication data is available
from the Library of Congress

ISBN   0 87830 206 9 (paper US)
ISBN   0 87830 205 0 (cloth US)

*This book is dedicated
to the teachers and students of Italia Conti's Acting Course
who took part in the development of these techniques*

Acknowledgements

The publisher gratefully acknowledges permission
to quote from the following:

The Birthday Party by Harold Pinter,
published by Faber and Faber Ltd (UK)
and Grove Press (US).

A Doll's House by Henrik Ibsen,
translated by Kenneth McLeish,
published by Nick Hern Books Ltd.

Oleanna by David Mamet,
published by Methuen Publishing Ltd (UK)
and Random House (US).

Sexual Perversity in Chicago by David Mamet,
published by Methuen Publishing Ltd (UK)
and Grove Press (US).

Contents

ACTING AND REACTING

Introduction

Like all art forms, the art of acting cannot be entirely quantified, nor reduced to scientific or logical principles, and even if it could, it is unlikely that this would create better actors. For this reason there has never been any volume published on acting which could claim to be a comprehensive step-by-step manual on how to do it. In fact, there are remarkably few books on the market which in any sense get to grips with the actor's process in the space. Writing down what they do seems to be something which few acting tutors get round to, which is why we still rely so heavily on Stanislavski and the pioneers of the American Group Theater.

The idea of being able to learn a creative skill like acting from a book may be an absurd one, but it is still a pity that so much of the knowledge and experience possessed by acting tutors remains hidden within their studios, and in many cases dies with them. It is generally agreed within the drama school world that there is a need for more practical books which outline and explain the processes of actor training and rehearsal. With this in mind I have written what I hope will ultimately be one among many such books, containing a combination of discourses, exercises and approaches which could accurately be described as 'tools' for you the actor to pick up, try out and use as you see fit.

It may be that you will take issue with some aspects of this book, but find others useful or inspiring. You may feel you can improve upon my ideas and make them your own. You may on the other hand consider that the entire volume is the direst heresy and fling it into the bin. That too is your choice.

There will never be universal agreement on how actors should be trained, and that is perhaps a good thing.

The driving force behind the book was my observation over a number of years that many trainee and professional actors appear to be working from the neck up rather than through the expressive body, and that they often don't seem to be relating or responding to each other in the performance space. As a teacher of acting in a well-known British drama school, I have spent many years working with colleagues to develop new approaches to actor training, which place emphasis on the body, the ensemble and the space, encouraging actors to view performance as a social and transactional process rather than the exploration of an actor's internal world.

If you are an acting teacher I imagine that much of this book will be familiar ground for you, but I hope you will find some of the exercises creative and useful. If you are a trainee actor then I hope it will help you in your quest to develop a personal philosophy and methodology within your craft, and to remain open to further new ideas and approaches throughout your career.

1

Stanislavski the Humanist

Everyone within the field of theatre owes an enormous debt of gratitude to Stanislavski, the Russian director and teacher who evolved the first 'system' of actor training. No-one could ever deny that he and his associates turned the craft of acting from a series of crude and self-aggrandising tricks into an elaborate and enlightened craft, which more than any other system of the twentieth century helped to raise the status of the actor from that of mountebank to creative artist. Stanislavski also created techniques for investigating and staging text which became the prototype for all modern approaches.

To this day there are still teachers proclaiming Stanislavski's System as the best way to train actors. To a greater or lesser extent, most drama schools still base their training on The System, and many of the other practitioners, such as Strasberg and Meyerhold, whose theories are also in common use, either trained under Stanislavski or were heavily influenced by him. Stanislavski's key works may have been re-examined and reworked a number of times in many different countries, but no-one has yet seriously challenged his supremacy.

It should never be forgotten, however, that Stanislavski was a man of his time, and his thinking reflects that time. To be fair to him, had he lived to the present day, it is very unlikely he would still be using his own early techniques, since he himself was constantly open to new ideas. Throughout his career, however, there were certain absolutes to which he adhered, and which we now have to challenge, because it is these absolutes which are partly responsible for the problems which arise in actor training today. Very few people actually working within the field of actor training have seriously considered the fundamental flaws in The System, or seen how inappropriate it is for training the kind of actor we expect today, and yet these flaws are very apparent, not just from the books which make up The System, but from Stanislavski's own work in the theatre.

Almost all of Stanislavski's methodologies were based on the attempt to manipulate the unconscious, whether through internal processes of thought and imagination or through physical action and sense memory. The idea was that the actor discovers during rehearsal the character's emotional journey through the play, and uses The System to rediscover that journey every night, the theory being that if the actor follows the pathway he has set for himself then his work will remain fresh and emotionally truthful even after fifty performances.

The fact that Stanislavski thought it necessary for the actor to create a fully rounded character and a coherent emotional journey before he actually steps onto the stage, probably owes much to the 'ego' culture which Stanislavski grew up with, and which pervades the acting profession to this day. We in the human race like to think of ourselves as complete, autonomous, essential beings with an identity somehow forged outside of the world we live in. We prefer not to regard ourselves merely as constructs of our culture, and we conveniently forget that our language, sign systems, ways of thinking, speaking, moving, feeling and decision-making are all for the most part culturally specific and the result of learned behaviour.

The erroneous perception of ourselves as 'stand-alone' characters with fixed identities and objective decision-making powers is a fantasy and an indulgence which throughout our culture is not merely allowed, but actively encouraged both in life and in much of mainstream drama. As actors, and as audience members, we can live out this fantasy through the drama by creating or experiencing characters who exist within the world of the play but are also totally embodied and conceptualised by the actor and therefore also exist outside of it. This illusion was fed by Stanislavski's System, which encouraged actors to 'build' their characters virtually single-handed. The end result of this is a theatre which is a giant metaphor and amplifier for humanist delusions. I, the audience member, see a character who is psychologically and emotionally 'great'; behind the character I see an equally 'great' actor; behind the actor I see a 'great' human being, and behind that, my own potential 'greatness' as a member of the human race. It is a satisfying process, but it is not real.

In fact the actor should be a very humble person, deeply aware of how subjective and vulnerable are our human egos and how far our so-called 'characterisations' depend on our spontaneous responses to one another in the moment. These responses cannot be prepared beforehand and we have little conscious control over them. There is really no such thing as a 'character' for the actor – what the audience sees as character is just the actor responding to other actors, albeit in different circumstances from those of his own life. If the actor appears to be a different character in each role he plays, it is because he has realised that it is circumstances and society which create character, and that his little ego is in itself just a social construct which he can let go of in the acting space. In other words, the actor merely needs to learn the lines, understand the given circumstances in their fullest sense and respond to what happens in the space. It is the *audience*, not the actor, who will then construct notions of who the character is, based on what they observe and how they understand it.

It is time that acting came to be seen for what it really is – a series of signs and indicators in the space which create the illusion of a person behaving in a certain way within a certain situation. Theatre and drama can be viewed as constructs which make use of the suggestibility and imagination of their audience to create illusory experiences whose purpose is in some way to reflect or comment upon life. It is the audience's observation of behaviour they can recognise and categorise, not their vague awareness of hidden psychological depths, which keeps their attention.

Within the drama schools, however, many of our actors are still trained to 'transform' themselves into psychologically rounded characters through introspective and self-absorbed internal exercises, in a way which makes them curiously inhuman and disconnected from the space and from each other. For generation after generation, actors have assumed that this is acting, and audiences who know no better have assumed they should admire it, which in turn has led actors to assume they are acting well. To challenge this curiously circular arrangement it is necessary to examine Stanislavski's ideas in the context of his life and social situation, so that the subjectivity of his assumptions can be exposed.

Stanislavski himself derived from the Russian *haute bourgeoisie*, not quite aristocrats, but wealthy manufacturers and landowners who to all intents and purposes lived as aristocrats, with country estates and massive wealth. Living in a country with a recent history of feudal slavery, where unimaginable poverty still reigned, the rich educated classes readily bought into a form of humanism which derived from capitalism and which placed emphasis on the essential nature of the individual. In other words, if I am at the top of the social ladder, speak well, recite poetry, have good manners and dress elegantly, this is because my soul is that of a higher being, not because I have been constructed by my family's wealth, refinement and power. Similarly, if you are a rough inarticulate peasant in rags, I may feel sorry for you, because it is also in my gift to feel such emotions, but like it or not, you are that way because you have a peasant's soul, and nothing can change that.

This philosophy naturally suited the ruling classes, because it vindicated their wealth and preserved their sense of status. It also meant that when the middle and upper classes wrote plays about themselves, they could place emphasis on the individual and his personal/emotional struggles rather than on the ways in which the social order constructs the individual and perpetuates the hierarchy. In this way they could avoid engaging with the emerging modernist discourses which challenged this essentialist position by showing how the human subject is not a coherent 'soul', but is a collection of behaviours which are learned and ingrained during the struggle to gain and maintain acceptance and status within the social order. On the lower end of the social scale these struggles might be mostly about simple hand-to-hand survival; at the upper end, where survival is not a daily issue, one might see people competing by building beautiful houses or wearing elegant clothes, or even by creating 'great' art.

It is unlikely that Stanislavski himself altogether agreed with the excesses of the Russian class system, or with the elitism of the rich, but, like many people of his class, he was able to identify social problems in terms of material issues of wealth and poverty, without questioning his own individualist philosophies or acknowledging that they were not universal and common to all people, but were also products of capitalist ideology and social conditioning.

The System, evolved from Stanislavski's collection of training manuals, places almost total emphasis on the individual mind, the individual's imagination and emotions, and the individual will. The concepts of 'the through-line of action' and of slipping seamlessly from one objective to the next, from one emotional point to another, all as part of a meticulously planned *mise-en-scène*, give us an impression of the individual as a coherent and independent whole, whose existence transcends the social environment within which he finds himself. Colin Counsell, who devotes a whole chapter of his book *Signs of Performance* to Stanislavski, remarks that:

> The audience . . . sees one complex psychology, a psychologically profound individual pursuing their desires; mind dictating actions according to their will. The audience is presented not with a character but with that particular character, the unique individual who feels, thinks and so acts in that singular way . . . The individual thus becomes the basic, given unit that the audience must use in its sense-making . . . [1]

If the individual is all-important, then the job of the actor must principally be to show the audience the psychological and emotional depth of that individual, so that the audience can marvel at the profundity of the human soul, and by proxy – because the individual is of their own sort – of the profundity of their own soul. The audience observes the character pursuing his objectives and negotiating the obstacles which the world places in his way, but they are not led to ask in what part of the social order those desires originated, or how the character comes to be constructed in that particular way, because they are offered the individual only as a non-negotiable whole.

Playwrights of the time tended to work from within the same humanist framework. The Norwegian dramatist Henrik Ibsen created a number of characters who found themselves at odds with their rigid social environment for the sole reason that it was in their personality to be so. The plays are well constructed and present coherent if at times obsessive personalities, whose desires and actions run contrary to accepted morality, throwing them into both internal and external conflict from which they seldom emerge alive. While Ibsen does critique the severity of the moral order (and occasionally the social order) and its lack of compassion for the wayward individual, the emphasis in these plays is on the inner turmoil of the individual, brought about by the clash between morality and desire. As an actor himself, Stanislavski was fascinated by the way in which Ibsen's characters seemed to reveal the 'human condition', and much of the early work on The System was related to his own attempts to realise these and other roles on stage.

Other playwrights, notably Anton Chekhov, wrote in a very different way. Chekhov wrote about characters who, precisely *because* they feel culturally dislocated and alienated, struggle to maintain a belief in their essential self and in most cases fail to do so, becoming steadily more and more comical and grotesque as the material world shifts and re-forms around them. Chekhov shows us the fragility of a people rocked by change over which they have little control, dependent on garbled fragments of ideology, philosophy and tradition from which they frantically try to construct an objective and coherent world view, as if they were merely observers of life rather than a part of it. The plays have the potential to show us that the human condition is culturally defined, human identity a construct, and the notion of humanity objectively observing itself an absurd illusion. What is interesting is that for the past century directors and actors have found ways of interpreting Chekhov's plays through a lens of psychological realism and presenting the characters as rounded individuals who, although distressed by their crumbling society, never lose their wistful integrity.

Stanislavski himself attempted in his productions to build Chekhov's central characters into tragic figures whose statuesque inner psyches are assailed by the traumatic unfolding of social and political change in turn of the century Russia but who remain tragically dignified to the end. It is no wonder that Chekhov grew increasingly dissatisfied with Stanislavski and the Moscow Art Theatre as the principal producers of his works, since his characters (especially in the later plays) have far more in common with the figures of *Commedia dell'Arte* than with those of the realist tradition. They are defined by their social mannerisms, their status games, and their futile attempts to make grand defining gestures. The only ones who could be said to have clear objectives are the servants, and those are (understandably) usually about social and economic betterment.

The realist theatre is of course an immensely powerful tool for supporting a humanist ideology, for the simple reason that it too is a *construct* masquerading as an *absolute*. The actor is able to enter the world of the play as an intact individual, with his objectives and emotional journey worked out beforehand, and to allow the events which take place in the theatre space to affect him only as far as he has previously agreed. Even if he dies at the end of the play, he does so with his individuality intact, and of course after his death the audience sees him return to the stage and bow, showing that this awesome personality really does exist outside of the world of the play!

Stanislavski evolved an acting methodology which firstly emphasised the construction of the character, though objectives, physical actions and external mannerisms; and secondly thrust that character as a ready-made whole into the theatre space, so that the audience could experience the character's (pre-ordained) journey but never question it or witness the actor being genuinely or unexpectedly affected by another actor. In rehearsal the actor was encouraged to generate from within much of what he needed to play the part. His imagination would create the world of the play and the 'magic if'; his affective memory would switch on the right emotions at the right moment; and his burning objectives would provide him with the energy to carry him through to the end. To an audience accustomed to an even grander and more self-consciously theatrical presentation of the individual offered by the 'heroic' acting of the nineteenth century, such performances must have seemed magically subtle in their portrayal of the psychological 'light and shade' of the character. It is unlikely they even noticed that very little of what an actor actually did in the space genuinely affected any other actor, or that most of the time the actors were not genuinely listening to one another, or more importantly, they were not observing in each other all the little involuntary non-verbal communicators which signify a person's social language.

Many of Stanislavski's 'descendants', including Lee Strasberg and Jerzy Grotowski, continued in their own ways to pursue the ultimate theatrical expression of the inner human psyche, like some invisible holy grail which is hidden from us by the mundaneness of the material world and of social convention. By contrast, another practitioner, Sanford Meisner, turned his attention to the simple chemistry of how people respond to each other when they are communicating. Unlike the more Brechtian schools of acting, Meisner was not so much interested in deconstructing our social gestures, but in letting the audience see them happening in minute detail, much as they do in real life. To achieve this he had to retrain his actors to respond to each other without censorship in the moment, so that what the audience would see was the involuntary response dictating how the text was spoken. In other words, instead of a scene being a series of intertwined prepared individual journeys it became an arena in which the actors could transact their social business for real, using each other's responses as the gauge of their status and acceptance, just as we do in life. The character is not particularly important as a total concept; the important elements are the unconscious *strategies* which the actor signifying the character employs in the space, and how he responds to the strategies of others. The rest is not important. If we are to see those strategies at work, however, then the actor has to give up two things – his conscious control of how the text is spoken, and his conscious control of the character's 'emotional journey' through the scene. It is no longer a case of the

actor imposing his 'will' in the space, but of the actor negotiating his way through the social environment and employing strategies which are chosen in the moment to deal with
what he encounters.

Meisner also places much less emphasis on the distinction
between the world of the play and the world of the theatre. If
we start by admitting that theatre is a construct, not real life,
we do away with the need to set up the pretence that it is real
life, either for the audience or for the actors. This means the
fourth wall disappears, and the actor can acknowledge that the
audience is there just as the wings and dressing rooms are
there. The world of the play does not need to exclude the
world of the theatre. This is something which Stanislavski,
within his absolutist school of thought, could not deal with.
For him there was either the world of the play or the real
world – you couldn't combine the two. You existed in either
one or the other, and if you chose the world of the play then
you had to shut out and deny the world of the audience.

In fact this is nonsense. In the twenty-first century we
know that we live our whole lives with one foot in our immediate reality and one foot in an imaginary world, or rather a
series of imaginary worlds created by television, media images,
computers and our own memory and fantasy. These worlds
do not exclude each other – they coexist. We allow them all to
be there simultaneously. It is our focus that shifts, and if we
are focused on one thing then the rest does not cease to be
there, it merely ceases to be important in that moment.

So we ask the actor to 'allow' all worlds to be present
within the theatre, but also to 'allow' himself to be absorbed
by the events and circumstances of one particular imaginary
world rather than the world of the audience and auditorium.
Once we have opened ourselves to this concept, then we are
free of the need to carry some imaginary picture of the
fictional world or of the 'character' around with us – we
merely allow it to be there. An actor should be responding
not to his imagination but to other people as he perceives
them; it is in his interaction with other people that we find
what Sanford Meisner calls 'the reality of doing'.

One might say that Stanislavski's era was one of extreme
arrogance, a time when human beings believed they could

really comprehend the complexities of their own psychology and the problems of their society and culture using only the conscious mind of the individual. This was the age of the great dictator, the superman and the pursuit of final absolute truth. It was the greatness of the human soul in adversity which Stanislavski sought to demonstrate, rather than the fragility and subjectivity of our identity. Nowadays much of our drama does not set out to offer eternal verities or grand messages; rather it seeks to capture droplets of human activity and distil them for our observation. It is not the grand eternal truth but the microscopic social truth which we seek in our drama, and such truths cannot be found by conscious analysis – only by allowing the process of human interaction to take place as organically onstage as it does in real life, albeit within different parameters.

It is time to leave Stanislavski behind, not without acknowledging his contribution to the evolution of the actor's art. It is time for our actors to stop searching for the elusive 'character' and understand that a character, far from being a comprehensible absolute, is something perceived in the moment through a series of both consciously and unconsciously generated signifiers. And it is time to train our actors to observe and respond to each other rather than following some internal pattern, night after night, often with deeply felt emotion, but without listening to anyone else on stage, and without allowing themselves to be affected by the unexpected. Emoting is not acting, reproducing is not acting. Reacting is acting.

2

Mamet the Modernist

Most actors are probably now familiar with David Mamet's *True and False*,[2] first published in the US in 1997. It is arguably the first book which actively takes on the hegemony of Stanislavski and Lee Strasberg within the Western drama tradition, deconstructing and demystifying the concepts which underpin these training methodologies, and dismissing them as unproductive and ultimately obstructive distractions from the actor's basic craft. It is a revolutionary book which has caused much consternation and controversy, not least among those providing actor training on both sides of the Atlantic.

Unlike the Stanislavskian practitioners, Mamet takes a modernist approach to the whole notion of 'character' and character preparation. Character, he argues, is an illusion in the mind of the audience, suggested by the fusion of the playwright's words with those aspects of the actor's personality revealed through behavioural signs in the moment:

> The actor does not need to 'become' the character. The phrase, in fact, has no meaning. There is no character. There are only lines upon a page. They are lines of dialogue meant to be said by the actor. When he or she says them simply, in an attempt to achieve an object more or less like that suggested by the author, the audience sees an illusion of a character upon a stage.[3]

This is very much in line with Colin Counsell's critique of Stanislavskian approaches to actor training, and it reinforces Counsell's challenge to the enduring myth of the actor 'creating' character, which has dominated our understanding of the actor's art since the end of the nineteenth century, and which we now have to try and get beyond.

Lee Strasberg's school of 'Method Acting', Mamet goes on to argue, is about pre-judging what a play should be communicating and then making sure that it does so. The problem with this, he contends, is that the actor is then placed in a position where any *real* reaction or involuntary human response in the space has to be censored and suppressed, because the actors are not trained to allow the natural and spontaneous response, only to summon up set feelings and emotions aimed at conveying a preconceived notion of character.

> We actors, being human, do not like the unexpected. If we encounter the unexpected onstage in front of people, we are apt to reveal ourselves. And formal academic education and sense memory and emotion memory and creative "interpretation" and all of these skills which are much more appropriate, finally, to the lectern than to the stage, are ways of concealing the truth of that revelation – of that moment.[4]

One of the problems with overturning the mythology and mystique of the 'great' actor who 'creates' psychologically profound characters, is that the whole acting profession's sense of self is built on that mythology. Acting is by any standards a precarious profession, not just because it is overcrowded and jobs are hard to come by, but because there is a sneaking suspicion among some industry professionals and members of the public that anyone can be an actor, without need for training or 'trade secrets'. As a result, many actors jealously guard their 'craft' and are happy to perpetuate the myth that taking on a role is difficult and takes months of careful study and preparation. Mamet pours scorn on these processes, suggesting that much of the actor's supposed preparation merely serves to create the illusion of depth and profundity, often at the expense of truth and clarity, by imposing unnecessary mental and emotional 'clutter' onto relatively simple transactional dialogue.

One of the biggest paradoxes associated with the global nature of film and television drama is that we are encouraged to worship world-famous actors as if they were gods, when the whole point of being an actor is to let us the audience see a human being's ordinariness, even when doing extraordinary things. If our most prominent actors are still so insecure they have to drape themselves in artistic and emotional mystique and cultivate moody inward-looking personalities or glamorous lifestyles, then it is clear that the profession has still not come of age. Its members are still not able to admit openly that the task of the actor is in essence remarkably simple – to learn the lines, to know what the play or screenplay is about and where this character fits into it, to know what the director wants, and then to read and respond in the moment without censorship. Actors who do this will stop trying to control their work, will become vulnerable and exposed, and will discover much in the moment, none of which they will ever need to reproduce, because there will always be another moment to respond to. More to the point, they will be believable, recognisable and truthful. This is Mamet's main point within *True and False*, and actors who have read it have variously responded with horror and fear, or with relief and joy. For some actors these straightforward statements negate their whole craft and life's work; for others they remove the chains and millstones that have held that craft back.

Mamet is of course reacting, with feelings of frustration and exasperation towards his own experiences of the American acting profession and training establishments. As a result *True and False* takes quite a radical stance on actor training, asserting that spending years studying at drama school really isn't necessary. In Mamet's view there is no need to train, or to study the text, or to rehearse. If the play is good, he contends, the words will speak for themselves, and if not, there is nothing the actor can do about it short of rewriting it.

It could be argued that Mamet has taken his anti-Stanislavskian position onto a level of antipathy towards the training process per se which risks being equally extreme and therefore equally unproductive. In trying to deconstruct what is dubious in actor training methodology, Mamet has perhaps 'thrown the baby out with the bath-water.' It is not as easy as it sounds for untrained actors just to pick up a text and 'act' without further ado. The error Mamet makes in positing the ultimate simplicity and therefore ease of what the actor does, is in incorrectly assuming that the actor is a) a blank page or unblocked neutral conduit for the playwright's words; b) in possession of sufficient knowledge about the world, past and present, and c) naturally endowed with all the physical and vocal faculties required to communicate successfully within the artificial world of the theatre or studio space. Anyone who has trained actors of whatever age knows this is simply not the case. Mamet deals somewhat glibly with the notions of voice and movement training, casually insisting that the actor must 'speak up, speak clearly, open yourself out . . . '[5] Such things are easier said than done, especially if the actor is to allow herself to be open and vulnerable to the moment in the way that Mamet and Meisner suggest. Furthermore, while actors might have no trouble understanding a modern western play about modern western characters written in relatively sparse colloquial language, there are other styles of writing where the actor's spontaneous rendition of the text may fail to communicate its potential, simply because the actor is not familiar enough with the language style and background. Not all actors can simply bring Shakespeare or a Restoration text off the page without study and practice, while other playwrights such as Chekhov have been consistently misunderstood by actors and directors alike for the simple reason that these actors and directors didn't know enough about the particular time and setting of the plays. Language and culture are inextricably intertwined; to comprehend the one is to begin to comprehend the other. Actors who try to understand a different kind of language purely in terms of their own culture will almost always miss the point. This is not to suggest that an actor should, for example, have to live in Nigeria for six months before taking a role in a Wole Soyinka play. But to know something of the society from which the play arose, to be aware of how Nigerians see their world and to recognise how the language reflects that, is surely the very thing that will enable the actor to understand the play and find ways of communicating the text to her audience.

Another problem of working without training is that the actor is not 'neutral' in terms of her physical and vocal mannerisms. The way we speak and move is at least partly due to social conditioning, and everyone has mannerisms and habits which dominate their responses within their own lives. An actor who has not been trained to move and speak differently will tend to come out with the same mannerisms over and over again, no matter what the role, and if these include a very tense upper body and a poorly supported voice, then she will have little success as an actor. For many of us, the pressures of modern life create in our bodies a certain tension and physical defensiveness, and these inevitably get in the way unless the actor is trained to work outside of her habits. We have to remember that an actor working in the space is not the same as a person seen in real life. She may be employing similar mannerisms, may be responding to what she encounters through the same physical systems, but she will be working in a distilled and heightened way, even if her aim is to appear as much like real life as possible. That is the nature of the actor's art, just as the playwright, however dedicated to reproducing real human dialogue, will not simply transcribe real speech, but will write in a way that excludes the irrelevant and heightens the significant.

Mamet also writes contemptuously about what he calls 'funny voices', by which one assumes he means anything that differs from the actor's own habitual vocal choices. Within Mamet's own plays, set for the most part in modern-day America, it might be that the narrow range of an actor's everyday vocal usage will suffice. It will hardly do for Restoration plays, or for Greek drama, or for a play set in the British Raj. But even in Mamet's own plays actors need astonishing vocal resources in terms of breath control, resonance and support, so that every little response is amplified and emotionally connected. What is more, actors have to learn to use a much wider range of physical responses in their work than they would ever employ in their lives. Our own gestures and habits will sometimes do (albeit in a modified and distilled form) when a drama is rooted in our own culture. Other cultures and other theatrical traditions have other physicalities, and even if the exact nature of these is lost in the mists of time, the language of the text will suggest physicalities which both fit with the language and make it comprehensible to a modern audience. It is up to the actor to inhabit these physicalities and make them her own. It should also be remembered that acting is not all about single actors playing single characters in broadly realist dramas. Acting work can also be based in the ensemble, with chorus work, physical theatre and very heightened physical and vocal expression. Actors need to be trained, not just to 'speak clearly' but to employ a range of physical and vocal skills which go far beyond those of everyday usage.

Somewhere between the total character creation of Stanis-lavski or Strasberg and the no-nonsense pragmatism of David Mamet is the space which modern actor training must seek to inhabit. Such training must endow an actor with the vocal and physical skills which both Stanislavski and Mamet insist on, must sweep away barriers, preconceptions and senti-mentality, must give knowledge and the ability to think, and must allow the actor to work in a responsive and uncensored way. This book is about training actors in a way which em-powers them to be the actors Mamet would employ – actors who know only what they need to know, who allow them-selves to be exposed in the space and who . . .

. . . deny nothing, invent nothing – accept everything, and get on with it.[6]

3

The Space Between

If actor training based on Stanislavskian principles tends towards individualism and excessive prescription, while at the other end of the scale Mamet advocates no training and a *laissez-faire* approach, then those looking to construct a new system of training will need to locate the *space between* these opposite viewpoints, and ask, 'how can we train in a way which gives actors a *craft* and a *process*, while at the same time allowing them to retain total spontaneity and be genuinely alive and responsive in the moment?' Much of the rest of this book is devoted to answering this question, but before we start to look at the practicalities of actor training, we need to be clear about the guiding principles and philosophies which underpin all the practical exercises and techniques, and which distinguish this approach to actor training from those which have gone before. Actor training is not an absolute, nor a clinical process, but on the other hand, neither should it be woolly and imprecise. A training programme may use a range of different teaching methodologies, but it should also have a central philosophy which unites all its strands and enables it to be clear about its aims and strategies. In the light of the previous two chapters, it should now be possible to sketch out the basic principles which underpin the actor's craft, and to create some sort of definition of what acting is and also what it isn't.

WHAT ACTING IS

Put simply, the job of the actor is to enter a space which has been designated as the acting space, and before an audience or a camera to speak scripted words, listen to other actors speaking scripted words, and respond physically and spatially to what happens, in a way which creates some kind of illusion for the audience that they are observing real people interacting within a set of real circumstances. This is usually on the understanding that both audience and actors have previously agreed this is what will happen, so that both are predisposed to allowing this process to occur. There are of course many forms of theatre and performance which do not use words or create dramatic narratives in this way, but it is probably safe to say that most of the drama we observe on stage or screen broadly adheres to this model.

The agreement which allows drama to take place in this way is in some ways a precarious one. The fictional world which the actors set up in the space depends entirely on the ability of both actors and audience to allow a constructed illusion momentarily to take precedence over the immediate realities of each person's everyday world. This illusion is of course fleshed out by the experience and imagination of each audience member. Indeed, the reason drama can take place at all is that our species has an inbuilt facility for extrapolating and conceptualising that which it cannot directly observe from that which it can. Using their own experience and memories, each audience member constructs from what is shown to them in the space a detailed and expanded notion of the fictional world whose outline has been signified to them by the actors. Where actors and audience have shared cultural signs and collective knowledge, the simplest of indicators can create in the imagination of the observer a highly detailed picture of the world of the play, complete with all its internal rules and social conventions. Actors do not necessarily need costume or props to create these pictures – in many cases just a handful of words will suffice. The experience and suggestibility of the audience does the rest. If two actors walk into a space with a certain physicality and one says 'Lunch on the terrace today, Jenkins' to which the other replies 'Very good, my lord', then so long as the accents and physicality accord in the audience's minds with the spoken words then most English-speaking audiences from all social backgrounds will probably be able to construct a picture of an English country mansion on a summer morning some time in the twentieth century from this brief exchange alone. If the same two actors enter with different physicalities and one says 'What is your quest, Sir Galahad?' to which the other replies 'I seek the Holy Grail', the same audience will have little difficulty in placing the exchange within an Arthurian legend, whether or not the actors are wearing armour and carrying swords.

The simple truth is that within any theatrical experience it is the audience which does most of the imaginative work, not the actor. The job of the playwright is to create a series of verbal indicators from which the audience will ultimately be able to construct a world and a narrative within that world. The job of the actor is to add vocality and physicality to that text so that those verbal indicators take on emotional and interactive dimensions, thereby adding further meaning and possibly counterpoint to the original text. While most texts invite new readings by a director or company, the job of the actor is not to weigh down their performance with psychological and emotional 'clutter', any more than the set designer needs to overload the space with irrelevant naturalistic detail. Actors who respect the text and work with it will usually reveal through their performance something new and interesting; actors who strain to be innovative and impose upon the text their own dubious character interpretations will fail to reveal anything but their own futile efforts.

EMOTIONAL OPENNESS

Audiences may be suggestible, and it is certainly the power of the audience's imaginations which lies at the heart of the theatrical experience, but an actor who sends out confusing or conflicting messages can lose the audience and arouse their disbelief as easily as the clear and truthful actor can win their trust. Confusion arises in the audience when they realise that what they are being *told* to observe and what they are *actually* observing are at odds with each other. The most obvious example is where an actor attempts to sign an emotion – grief for example – through shaking shoulders, hunched body and sobs, but because the emotion is not actually being felt by the actor, the audience detects (all too easily) that although they are being asked to believe in the presence of the emotion, all they can actually observe is the actor's efforts to sign the emotion. The reason audiences can detect such empty demonstrations is that they have an innate capacity for picking up genuine emotional signals from the physical and vocal behaviour of others, and where these signals are not present, this can be detected regardless of outward demonstrations.

For you the actor, this is usually the biggest demon – the need to feel 'genuine' emotion where the text demands it. This problem is aggravated by your awareness of the *need* to express emotion in a truthful and believable way, which leads to anxiety and fear and, ironically, to further blockage. So many actors panic at the thought of having to hit a particular emotional level at a certain point in the play, convinced that they won't be able to do it, and anticipating the dreaded moment for several pages before it happens, which means they are unable to stay in the moment and thus miss any chance they may have had of allowing the moment to occur organically!

Yet an emotional moment must happen organically, and it must be part of the interaction which the audience has been observing, not some contrived outburst which you have found in yourself outside of the moment. Digging around in your own past to discover emotional responses which can be safely accessed and expressed is a dangerous and inexact science. Even if you can find 'safe' pathways through which to express emotion, these will not make you emotionally open, because your emotional 'vocabulary' will continue to be internally contrived and disconnected from the actual mo- ment. You become emotionally open by being physically open, through breathing and physical release which in turn leads to mental and emotional openness. Much of early training should be devoted to exercises which facilitate this release and free up your body and breath, so that you become accustomed to maintaining relaxation and openness even in moments of stress.

What you need to recognise, however, is that there is a strong symbiotic relationship between the mind and the body. A closed mind will always inhibit the body, just as a tense and held body will inhibit thought patterns. The first thing you need to do is 'let go' of all the defence mechanisms and safety barriers with which you arrive at drama school. In effect this means you have to dispense with the luxuries of fixed beliefs, closed thinking and habitual responses. It is the duty of any course of training to call to your attention those aspects of your personality which have been constructed, often through your teenage years, by social conditioning and personal experience, and to encourage you, in your own time, to hold open to question everything which you previously considered to be absolute in your life.

It should be emphasised, however, that this is not an exercise in indoctrination, nor is it intended to strip trainees of their most dearly held beliefs. Take for instance an actor who arrives at drama school with a strong Christian faith. Any personal faith which is not open to challenge or questioning soon stops being a faith and becomes a dogma or an obsession. The more ideas and points of view the actor can take on and consider, even if these at first appear to challenge their beliefs, the stronger their faith can potentially become. Anyone who defends their beliefs dogmatically and shuts their ears to other ideas is clearly worried about the fragility of that faith. By contrast someone who can take on and consider all new ideas, and adjust their thinking accordingly, has real courage and real faith. It is only those who do not fear attack who need no defences.

Sadly drama school all too often fails to open up the minds or the bodies of its trainees. The mythologies which circulate within schools often lead actors to believe only in a dog-eat-dog world with no room for generosity or openness, while the sheer anxiety and fear of failure leads to still more tension and suspicion. Many actors come to blame their training and their teachers when they feel frustrated and useless, as of course they will from time to time. For this reason it is very important that a course of training, like the actors it serves, constantly questions itself and is seen to do so. Furthermore, it must have a coherence, a philosophy and an underlying set of principles which can be communicated, discussed and questioned. It is unreasonable to ask you to put yourself on the line and to trust your training if what you are signing up to is a confused and random set of skills and ideas, which lacks a basic philosophy, whose teachers do not communicate with each other, and whose fundamental incoherence is obscured only by mystique and jargon.

TRUST AND ACCEPTANCE

Although it may be up to the drama school to facilitate your mental and physical journey, it is up to you, the actor, to place trust in your training through the following principle, which is: 'first *do* what is required, then ask questions'. In other words, follow the instructions of the tutor without defensiveness or reservation, find out where that leads, and then see if you need to ask questions. Acceptance of this principle is an important part of the training – you must learn by experiencing, not by asking beforehand what you are supposed to be experiencing. For you this is the difference between the 'yes' mentality and the 'yes, but . . . ' mentality – to learn to accept.

If you submit to the training and begin to think, breathe and move in a released and unblocked way, you will automatically find the capacity to affect others and be affected by them on whatever emotional level the text requires. You should never forget, however, that in the moment your reactions will often emerge not from your conscious mind but from the unconscious, which means you may be surprised by your own responses, or even simply not remember them when you come out of the space. As with all art forms, there is an element of your work which will always remain outside your conscious control. This does not mean, however, that you should work in a random or undisciplined way. The freedom and spontaneity which you can enjoy in the moment is directly proportionate to your confidence in the basic parameters of the training exercise, rehearsal or production, and your ability to do, without thinking, that which is required of you.

What you actually *do* as an actor in the space is a combination of the *fixed* and the *spontaneous*. The fixed elements can include the nature of the space, the shape of the set, the words of the text, the stage directions, the director's instructions, your understanding of the physicality or social customs of the play's setting, and your previous decisions about the particular vocality or physicality of the character. Taken together these make up the *given circumstances* of the performance. Unlike the Stanislavskian definition of given circumstances, this definition includes *all* circumstances which set the parameters for the actor's performance, not just the fictional circumstances of the character in the play. Again, the character is not seen as separate from the actor, nor is the world of the theatre separate from the world of the play. The actor exists in both worlds, and the two worlds overlap both with each other and with the actor's own personal world.

SETTING THE BOUNDARIES

You do not need to worry about the fixed elements within your performance, nor do you need to seek motivations for doing what has to be done. Many of the fixed elements will arise in rehearsal and be fixed by the director simply because they work and are clear. In a Brecht production, for instance, the director may be keen to find a character's 'social gestus' – a series of gestures and actions which reveal the character's social status and state of mind at specific points in the play. While the director may initially let these gestures emerge organically from rehearsal exercises, having once found clear and effective gestures, you may be asked to retain these in your performance because they serve the production as a whole. Some actors worry about being asked to perform an action over and over again, assuming that if they cannot find their 'motivation' for doing it in the moment, the action will be 'faked'. The answer to this is simple. People spend most of their lives doing actions which they have done hundreds of times before, without worrying about their motivation. If we are clear what has to be done, we can do it without thinking, and in the moment of doing it, it becomes natural for no other reason than we *consented* to do it. The only thing which makes an action appear faked is the actor doing it with reluctance. In other words, if you worry about motivations you create your own obstacles. Once again, the rule is *do* first, ask why afterwards.

ARTISTIC FREEDOM

Actors also worry that the fixed elements of a production will stifle their creativity. Nothing could be further from the truth. Freedom – and that includes artistic freedom – is a relative concept. Freedom without context is meaningless, and it is the parameters set by the fixed elements which create the greatest liberation for the actor, who is then free to play in the space between. The most wooden performances happen when an actor is standing in a space without any idea of what to do with their body. Robbed of structure the actor freezes up, unable to find a direction, an activity, a way forward. Too much freedom causes fear and confusion, and these are the actor's worst enemies. Give the same actor some structure – an activity, an aim, even an image to work with, and they will relax and get on with it. The most creative performances of all can sometimes take place within the tightest boundaries, because in the space between the boundaries you feel secure enough to take the greatest risks and be truly spontaneous.

The greatest skill you can acquire as an actor is to accept that which is fixed without worrying about it, and to work within the space created by the fixed parameters. Unfortunately, playwrights and directors often make the awful mistake of trying to set parameters and boundaries in places where they should not be set, and where they can genuinely stifle the actor's creativity. Where this occurs the actor should have the courage and conviction to challenge it. David Mamet suggests that when an actor reads a play she should take a pencil and cross out all stage directions which relate to the actor's emotional responses or states of mind. It is worrying how often playwrights assume they should be in control not just of the dialogue and basic stage directions, but of the actor's whole emotional journey. George Bernard Shaw, for example, prefaces almost every line of his plays with an adjective telling the actor what tone to use when speaking it, or what response they should have to the previous line. This kind of prescriptive writing may work for the Stanislavskian actor, but for the modern actor it is anathema. The playwright may tell you what to say and to some extent what to do physically, but they may not tell you how to feel. You are not there to reproduce, puppet-like, every intention of the playwright. Your job is to read the text, understand its basic meaning, and then to work in the space with the other actors to find not one, but many ways of playing it.

THE ACTOR'S LANGUAGE

If the early part of your training should be about release, openness and acceptance, then the next part needs to be about extending your physical and vocal vocabulary so that your body can be effectively used as a signifier for the widest possible range of characters and archetypes. Voice and Movement training require the actor to explore everything from the most specific and minute gestural detail to the wildest abstraction. Very early on in your training, however, you will learn to take on new and unfamiliar physicalities and vocalities which relate specifically to the social and personal circumstances of a particular character, and to make these your own. This can be anything from adopting heightened Received Pronunciation for an Oscar Wilde play, to finding the suspicious and watchful gestures of a nineteenth-century pickpocket, or the bent-over posture of the *Commedia dell'Arte* archetype of *Arlecchino*.

Without these vocabularies you will confuse your audience. This brand of confusion arises when your physical or vocal signs do not tally in the audience's mind with the meanings offered by the text itself. If you use a rather casual twenty-first-century physicality and vocality in a play, or characterisation which demands something more precise and heightened, you will fail to serve the text and will create a mismatch between the text and the acting. This will severely compromise the audience's experience of the play. Dropped consonants, repetitive rhythms and falling inflexions can betray a lack of ownership of the words and the thoughts, quite apart from your lack of grasp of the style of the text.

Among some actors there is a reluctance to work at a 'heightened' level, which leads to work of low vocal and physical energy. When questioned, actors will often express surprise that their work is regarded as imprecise or low in energy, or they will admit to being terrified of 'going over the top' (OTT). It can take a while to convince the new trainee that the opposite is the case, and that your energy levels would need to go up by a factor of about two hundred to run the risk of being OTT! In fact it is extraordinarily difficult for you to be OTT provided you keep breathing and work off the other actors. Even very strong physical and vocal work will seem in proportion if it is supported by good physical and vocal technique and arises organically from the scene. An audience will accept anything it can understand.

You will need to work with high energy from the early stages of training. Although the tutors may have to rein back work which is taking you into unsafe physical or vocal usage, you should get into the habit of making big offers in the space from the start, so that it quickly becomes second nature, and you avoid falling into patterns of self-consciousness or anxiety about how your offers will be received. You should set the tone for yourself in the first few weeks of training, otherwise you will find it hard to change later.

In essence, then, you are learning to *give* and to *receive*. At the outset you concentrate on unblocking the conduits in and out of your mind and body; after that you learn how to give appropriately – the right quality at the right moment, for which you need hard work and still more openness. If you can learn to be humble, generous and accepting, you will be halfway to being an actor. If you remain defensive, arrogant and selfish, you will get nowhere.

Until the initial work of 'opening up' physically, vocally, emotionally and intellectually, has taken place, the rest of the training cannot really happen. In the second stage of training you acquire the skills which help you negotiate the diverse nature of the profession. You learn to handle Shakespeare and other complex texts; you master microphone and camera technique; you extend your physical and vocal vocabulary to encompass the most extravagant characterisations or ensemble work. If you enter these advanced stages of training with a closed mind or body, you will experience nothing but frustration and despair. It is a deeply unpleasant experience for tutors to watch their trainees struggling in this way, but ultimately there is little that can be done for an actor who has put up defences against the training, especially if you are blaming your tutors and the course for the way you are feeling. My advice to you as you begin your course of training is this: 'Expect the training to be life-changing, hold onto nothing, embrace change, anticipate nothing, breathe.'

4

Transactional Improvisation – Part One

Nothing happens out of a context, and that includes actor training. The context in which drama schools accept (mostly) young people, with all their hang-ups, preconceptions, prejudices and fears, and without very much knowledge or experience to counter these, is at best a difficult one. We live in a world which is increasingly fragmented, and where reality depends largely on where you are standing. There is too much going on in our society in too many different ways, for us to make grand unequivocal statements about ourselves through our drama. The best we can do is to accept the complexity of our situation and create theatre which encourages its audiences to think about and to re-evaluate their own opinions and viewpoints, with the aim of discouraging 'fixed' thinking within our shifting world.

In theory this should be a wonderful thing for theatre. You, the new generation, should be coming into the drama schools buzzing with the sheer freedom of it all. Theatre and drama, at least in theory, have never before been so liberated from performance conventions, moral and political constrictions and internal hierarchies. For the actor starting drama school, however, the reality is sadly very different. Where there are no absolutes we try to create them, and the more elusive they become the more aggressively we defend them. Where society sets no parameters for us we create our own internal boundaries and barriers which are less visible than clear social parameters and therefore harder to identify and challenge. With fewer universally agreed standards for us to adhere to or to kick against, we grasp at half-formed ideas and statements in our search for certainty and for a belief-system through which to define ourselves.

This is nobody's fault, of course. The information we need in order to comprehend and come to terms with our social existence may not be actively withheld, but it is swamped in such a deluge of 'white noise' information that many students find it almost impossible to distinguish between that which is constructed by the media and that which is really happening. It is not difficult to equip students with analytical powers, and to adjust the flow of information so that the trivial and the significant are differently presented – that is the first duty of education in any event; what is more difficult is getting you to accept that the contradictions and conflicts apparent in any examination of world events do not lie outside of you, but have a direct connection with you as members of the human race and of human society.

In this context, the moment we begin to dismantle the structure of your fixed set of beliefs about yourselves and the world you live in, we find insecurity, panic and despondency. Yet we have to dismantle it, otherwise you will never be able to do more than 'pretend'.

This, then, is our first job – to confront you with the scary knowledge that not only do terrible things happen in the world, but the aspects of human nature which bring about those events are present in each and every one of us, and the only reason we are able to sit comfortably in our nice complacent little worlds pretending we do not have the potential to commit atrocities ourselves is that we are not exposed to that level of pressure, need or desperation.

You cannot afford, at least in the acting space, to hold fixed moral views about anything, or to be judgemental of others. You should only be interested in why people behave as they do, not in whether it is right for them to do so. You need to understand that the concepts of 'rightness' or 'wrongness' are entirely subjective and depend on where you are standing at the time. You can explore morality, but you have to see it for what it is – a series of rules which apply at a particular time in a particular place under particular circumstances.

However difficult the process, once you have accepted, without judgement or moralising, that every possible facet of human behaviour is genuinely within your scope, and that within the acting space all these facets may be explored, the permission this gives you is boundless. However, it is useless to demand cruelty, violence, passion, despair or whatever from you out of context. The extremes of human behaviour belong to the extremes of human experience – outside of those contexts they are without meaning and without consequence. This is where Transactional Improvisation (TI) comes in.

Transactional Improvisation is a way of seeing the world which allows us to explore the processes of human trans-action on both a literal and symbolic level while steering clear of 'psychobabble' and Freudian deconstruction, and while also removing all element of objective moral judge-ment from human activity. Within Transactional Improvisa-tion everything is possible and all motivations are found in the immediate situation. TI keeps you focused and dynamic, and stops you getting stuck in your head.

The first rule of TI is that it contains no moral or value judgements. There are no positive or negative actions; there is only the balance on which all things are weighed and the consequences of each action, which must be dealt with. You are taught that at every level of interaction choices are defined by a process of negotiation which culminates in the moment of doing. Everything which affects that moment, including all the given circumstances, are contained within the terms of the transaction and are definable as such.

Transactional Improvisation starts from the idea that each individual within a pair, a family, a group or a society, is engaged in a constant and ongoing process of 'jostling' for status within that group, sometimes slowly and gradually, sometimes quickly and urgently, depending on the dynamic of the situation. All human interaction, fundamentally, comes back to this relatively primeval process, which of course is what all drama is about. Within a play like *Glengarry Glen Ross*,[7] it is possible to see the jostling for supremacy very clearly at work; within a Chekhov play the process may be concealed under layers of poetically expressed feeling, but it is still there.

We all know that groups of chickens, among other animals, operate simple 'pecking orders', based largely on physical strength and aggression. To some degree human status is also defined in this uncomplicated way, but within today's complex set of societies and social groupings, status is achieved through many other forms of transaction, and in the modern age the status of the individual is perpetually being redefined, often in terms of possessions and sexual attractiveness, but also in terms of winning or losing face through verbal or physical stand-offs. Most of the traditional hierarchies which once characterised feudal or class-driven societies have either been swept away or marginalised within western urban society, so that in each moment individuals are expected to renegotiate their status, with their parents, partners, children, employers, employees and friends and with total strangers.

Like any form of negotiation, these transactions can only take place through a process in which one person offers something to another, which is either accepted or rejected. Within human interactions these offers can be abstract and conceptual, and for that reason we often fail to interpret them correctly. For instance, if one person steps on another's toe in a train, the transaction might go something like this:

PERSON 1. Sorry. (*Offers remorse and empathy, but not very much and demands closure.*)

PERSON 2 (*in pain and annoyed by the paucity of the offer*). That really hurt! Why don't you look where you're putting your big feet? (*Offers pain and annoyance and demands much more remorse and empathy.*)

PERSON 1 (*startled and worried by the level of annoyance*). Look, I'm really sorry. I'm such a clumsy idiot. (*Offers remorse and self-deprecation and demands forgiveness and closure.*)

PERSON 2 (*mollified by the level of this offer*). It's all right. (*Accepts the offer and fulfils the demand.*)

At the point of acceptance, the transaction is over and it is unlikely that either party will attempt to engage further with the other, at least not on this matter. In this case, Person 1 makes an offer, and Person 2 makes him see there is an element in the transaction (in this case the pain felt in the foot) which Person 1 had failed to take into account. Person 2 is prepared to reveal to Person 1 the precise extent of that pain, and this enables Person 1, who is anxious to achieve closure, to expose his culpability in the matter. The price has been paid and the deal is done.

However, it is possible that the transaction might have gone differently:

> PERSON 1. Sorry. (*Offers remorse and empathy, but not very much and demands closure.*)
>
> PERSON 2 (*in pain and annoyed by the paucity of the offer*). That really hurt! Why don't you look where you're putting your big feet? (*Offers pain and annoyance and demands much more remorse and empathy.*)
>
> PERSON 1 (*rattled and defensive at what seems a disproportionate response*). Well you shouldn't have stuck your bloody feet out into the gangway, should you? (*Offers defensiveness and demands closure.*)
>
> PERSON 2 (*outraged at this adding of insult to injury*). Just fuck off, you bloody elephant! (*Rejects the offer and offers raw aggression.*)
>
> (PERSON 1 *does not react.*)

Here too the transaction is probably over, since it is unlikely that either party will try to continue negotiating a peaceful settlement. In this case Person 1 refuses to pay the cost of the closure, and instead demands closure anyway as compensation for the insult. Person 1 now has the option of shifting the conflict to a verbal or physical war-zone, in which no mutual accommodation is possible – only the defeat of one of the parties. Person 1 decides against this option, and an uneasy closure is achieved, in which fear of open conflict (cold war style) holds the parties in a sort of balance.

A third, (but extremely unlikely) option would be for Person 2 to accept Person 1's anger and defensiveness, and thereby expose his own failure and thoughtlessness in having left his feet in the gangway. In this case, the conversation might run thus:

> PERSON 1. Sorry. (*Offers remorse and empathy, but not very much and demands closure.*)

PERSON 2 (*in pain and annoyed by the paucity of the offer*). That really hurt! Why don't you look where you're putting your big feet? (*Offers pain and annoyance and demands much more remorse and empathy.*)

PERSON 1 (*rattled and defensive at what seems a disproportionate response*). Well you shouldn't have stuck your bloody feet out into the gangway, should you? (*Offers defensiveness and demands closure.*)

PERSON 2 (*withdrawing annoyance and offering culpability*). Yes, you're right, I should have tucked my feet in.

But this offer is never made, because Person 2 feels this is too great a price to pay for no apparent gain, and can see nothing to be gained from making further demands.

The decisions the parties make within these scenarios are defined within Transactional Improvisation as a reckoning up between what is offered by the other person, and what it will cost us (in terms of exposure and loss of status) to accept the offer and fulfil their demand. If the two balance, the transaction can take place, if not, negotiation continues to the point where either an accommodation is reached or both parties recognise there is no possible accommodation which can be reached in that situation.

Another example might be someone who has feelings of sexual desire for a friend, but is not able to offer their desire (and demand it in return) for fear that by exposing that desire they risk weakening their status within the friendship, possibly to an extent which the friendship cannot sustain. In order for them to make this offer, either the level of desire would have to be so great that it outweighed the risk, or the risk would have to become smaller, perhaps through the other person giving some hint or indication that the desire was reciprocated.

Transactional Improvisation works through giving clear and precise names to the abstract qualities that form these non-material transactions, and making the act of locating and offering these abstract qualities the focus of all inter-action within the space. This is in marked contrast to identifying and performing action verbs.[8] The act of doing something to someone can be devoid of real significance, but the act of offering something you have and demanding something in return cannot, because if something is not genuinely offered it cannot be genuinely accepted.

The other key feature of TI is that within a training situation it *actively uses the real group relationships and dynamic* to create situations, so that the participants are confronted not with tenuous and remote fictions within their improvisations, but with real issues, which become fictional only by the process of *foregrounding*.

TI Exercise 1   The 'What-I-Am' Game

One actor in a group is asked to make a statement about themselves, something which they believe to be true, in the form of 'I am a ... person'. For example, one actor might say 'I am an insecure person', a statement which arises from a combination of how the actor generally perceives herself and how she is feeling in that moment. In the normal run of events, a statement of this kind might pass unnoticed – it would be unlikely to excite much opposition. However, as part of the exercise we now choose to examine that statement, and to find a different response.

We start with the assumption, which is one of the basic precepts of TI, that every line of text, either scripted or improvised, makes an *offer* and a *demand*. The offer is what I am prepared to give you; the demand is what I expect in return. In simple shopping terms this is easy. '*Can I have a pint of milk, please?*' spoken within the context of a shop offers money and demands milk. '*I am an insecure person*', on the other hand, is a more complex transaction, in which the nature of the offer is not immediately clear, although the demand probably is. The demand, if you think about it, is almost certainly going to be along the lines of *special treatment* or *exemption from responsibility*, or even *reassurance*. In other words, that person is asking for special consideration from the whole group. Put like that, it seems quite a big demand. To fulfil it the group will have to give up its right to say what it thinks, and give up the assumption of equality and parity between all its members, presumably until the insecurity has been dealt with at some unspecified time in the future. Of course, the group could pretend to accept the offer without actually doing so, but that would negate the whole transaction. It is from such 'non-transactions' that bad acting is made.

From this point the other actors within the group, while they can observe and express themselves individually, agree to act and make decisions as a body, with everyone working for the common cause. If the group as a whole is looking seriously at fulfilling the demand of the individual to be accepted as an *insecure* person, then they need to know exactly what the nature of the offer is. Although the text is fixed, the offer is not. The offer could be one of several things, and the group will need to look closely to see precisely what it is. It could be *insecurity*, as the statement implies, but it could equally be *egocentricity*, or it could be *certainty*, if the statement is made with enough conviction. At its most paranoid extreme, a line like this could be offering *violence or menace*. What the group reads as the offer will depend on the actor delivering the line. The group will then have to decide whether the offer is acceptable. If the group can genuinely see the insecurity, it may decide to accept the offer rather than risk being held responsible for upsetting someone or exposing in itself qualities of cruelty or unkindness. In this case the group will also perceive how much it *costs* the speaker to make the statement, in terms of personal exposure and risk of rejection.

On the other hand if all the group can see is a crude attempt at manipulation, it will most likely reject the offer because it does not wish to increase the speaker's power within the group. To accept that offer would expose the group's gullibility and credulity. Similarly, if the group sees strength and certainty, it will not believe in the *insecurity*, since we usually equate insecurity with doubt and fear.

The 'group' in this case means everyone. If there is even one dissenting voice, then the group as a whole must agree that the offer is unacceptable, and proceed to the next stage of the exercise.

The group places the statement, with its inherent offer and demand, at the centre of the space, and thereby at the

centre of its world, making this particular transaction
between the individual and the group the most important
issue, indeed, making the group's definition of itself and the
individual dependent on the outcome of the transaction.

This kind of *foregrounding* of an issue lies at the heart of all
acting, and is something which human beings do naturally at
all times. It does away with the need for fourth walls or any
other such artificial concepts. It is the simple process of
'prioritisation' which means that in certain circumstances we
reorder the relative importance of issues within our lives. A
good example is the driver who despite having his four-year
old child in the back of the car, gets into a 'road-rage' conflict
with another motorist which makes him drive recklessly and
place the child at risk. If in a calm moment that driver were
asked which took greater priority, the life of his child or the
issue with the other motorist, he would of course place the
child's welfare so far above the road rage incident that the
two would simply not exist on the same plane of compara-
bility. Yet the fact would remain that in a particular moment,
with a particular stimulus, his 'road-rage' was *foregrounded*,
and prioritised over the life of his child. This is the point in
most discussions where society's moral censure takes over,
and the driver is damned out of hand for his feckless and
irresponsible behaviour. In TI, however, we recognise that
our moral repugnance must be placed to one side, and that it
is only through understanding and participating in the act of
reprioritisation that we can allow ourselves fully to enter the
world of any improvisation or play.

> The group then 'reprioritises' the individual's statement 'I
> am an insecure person', so that it becomes a potential
> threat to group unity and equality. To crush the individual
> outright would be to expose the group's intolerance, and
> of course ironically would heighten the individual's reason
> for being insecure. Instead the group appoints a 'champion'
> whose job is either to force the individual to withdraw the
> statement, or to force the individual to offer enough to the
> group to enable them to accept it. The individual and the
> champion stand in the space with the rest of the group
> round the edge. The line 'I am an insecure person' now

becomes the actor's sole text. It can be spoken to the champion or to other members of the group, as many times as the individual wishes. The champion listens, sees, and responds each time to what he sees, using the line 'I see a ... person' (e.g. 'I see a manipulative person'). The champion's line must always be formulated in this way, but the adjective can change as his perception of the individual changes.

The individual's statement, and the champion's responses to it, become a conversation, and it is through the dynamic of that conversation that the individual must work. It is essential that the individual find the truth of the statement, not just in himself, but also in the immediate situation. When actors are new to TI, the tendency will often be to use crude manipulation tactics, disconnected gestures and fake emotion to convince the champion. It doesn't take long for the group and the individual to realise that none of these tactics works. Self-conscious manipulation is remarkably easy to spot, because it signs itself through an unsupported voice and uncentred body.

Eventually, often by going round in circles and getting very frustrated, the individual realises two things: firstly, that *he has to work off the champion and the group*, and secondly, that *it is better for an actor to give in than to be untruthful*. In order to make the statement truthfully, the individual must be able to find insecurity in the situation as it is, and truthfully to express it through the text. If he cannot find it, he *must* submit, and give up his ownership of the statement. This is the point where the individual realises that he is not, after all, insecure in this situation, and the champion's challenge is true. The individual must then end the conversation by agreeing with and echoing the champion's last statement, stating (for example): *'You're right, I am a manipulative person.'* What he is saying, in effect, is that he is unable to locate and expose his insecurity within that situation. What he is *not* saying is that he has never been nor will never feel insecure. It just isn't what's happening *now*, and the actor needs to learn that it is always what he can offer *now* which matters. Ironically, of course, it might be at the point where the individual gives in that the champion does finally see and recognise his insecurity.

[41]

During the process, any one of the champion's response lines may trigger off huge amounts of insecurity in the individual, so that by working off his opponent, the individual may find, and offer, all the insecurity he needs to make the statement. If this happens, and the champion sees the insecurity, *he* must submit by saying *'You're right, you are an insecure person'*, in which case he has submitted on behalf of the whole group, who must then take the consequences.

The exercise can then be repeated for each member of the group. Each one makes a statement about themselves, and each statement is analysed and challenged according to its nature and delivery. Examples of these statements from my own sessions include 'I am a friendly person', 'I am a passionate person' and 'I am a determined person'. In each case the group demanded of the individual that within the context of the space the quality was located and expressed in a way that the champion could believe in and accept it.

I have found that through their experience of the *self-knowledge game* actors realise the following:

1 That to make any statement convincingly you have to find the truth of the statement not just in a vague and general way, but within and through the precise moment that the statement is made.

2 That having found that truth, it must be offered outwards, not seen as a reason to block and constrain the breath and emotions.

3 That every statement, however bland or commonplace it may seem in itself, can be 'reprioritised' to form the centre of an issue or conflict which becomes entirely absorbing to the participants, and in which they can have a massive personal investment.

In Transactional Improvisation terms, the exercise is very simple. In order to get the group to fulfil the demand(s) the individual must locate and reveal his insecurity. There is a cost to this, which is that to offer insecurity he must expose his vulnerability, at the risk of being hurt or emotionally trampled on. The payoff, however, is the group's recognition and acceptance of this insecurity, and the fulfilment of the demand. At this point we need to consider how power and status operate within human society. We are accustomed to believing that someone who appears to be happy, strong and confident is in fact also powerful. Perhaps they are, but the person who is genuinely weak and unhappy and constantly reminds people of this fact, ironically wields a different and perhaps more insidious control over others. For the actor, defensiveness is rarely a potent tool – openness on the other hand can be extremely so.

Actors are often suspicious when they come to drama school. You may have heard myths about being 'broken down' and humiliated, which may lead you to start the course secretly determined to do nothing without first knowing precisely why, and to offer nothing unless you are sure of the return. Transactional actors, however, come to understand that to take risks, to *gamble*, is a key element of all transactions. Every transaction we enter into carries an element of risk, and if we were not prepared to accept that risk we would never transact anything. A meal we buy in a restaurant might not be to our taste; someone we marry might have an affair with someone else; our new DVD player might be stolen. Our society attempts to remove as much of that gamble as possible with insurance policies, pre-nuptial agreements and consumer guarantees, with the result that we have become very intolerant of risk, trying constantly to minimise and predict it, always working to avoid paying the cost of a gamble which goes wrong. We are a society which hates paying up. Insurance underwriters try to wriggle out of their commitments; politicians often no longer resign when they mess up; and actors come to drama school saturated in a culture of 'no-risk'. In TI, however, there are no guarantees. One of the first things an actor needs to learn is to offer what he has in each moment, however risky that might be and however unsure he is that it will be accepted. Later in the training he can learn to make more specific and subtler offers, but to begin with he just needs to take risks.

Having said that, TI exercises should always be conducted in an environment of trust and mutual support. Actors who make themselves vulnerable and exposed in the space need first to have confidence that however challenging an exercise may turn out to be, the underlying ethos of the session and the underlying motivations of the group are positive and educative, not manipulative or oppressive. It is the responsibility of the tutor to ensure that all individuals feel safe within the group before embarking on these next exercises, and it is your right as an actor to withdraw from any exercise if you genuinely feel that any individual within the group is abusing the permissions of the space.

TI Exercise 2   The 'What-I-Know' Game

A variation on the first TI exercise is where the group nominates an individual and sends her out of the room. In her absence the group has to decide on a statement which the individual will have to make to the group on her return. The statement is defined as 'the statement which the individual needs to make about herself or about the group, in order to move on as a person and as an actor.'

These statements are not always obvious, and their nature can vary hugely from individual to individual, according to how the group sees them. What needs to be made clear is that the statements are not *true*, any more than the statement 'the world is a beautiful place' is unequivocally true. It merely has an *element* of truth in it, which the actor needs to confront and explore rather than resist. For instance, an actor might be the kind of person who is superficially nice and caring, but the group suspects that there isn't much substance to this. In that case her statement might be 'I don't give a shit about any of you'. Another actor might be trying too hard in classes, being too keen, too frenetic, too intense. His statement might be 'I have no talent.'

In both of these instances the statements are what the group perceives as the one thing which the individuals in question are reluctant to admit even to themselves, and which their everyday conduct is designed to conceal or obscure. In the same way as we did away with the concept of 'naturalness' in human behaviour, so we can now also do away with the concept of 'truth' as an absolute. As an actor you need to be truthful only to the extent that in the moment of saying or doing something you are embracing, within your mind and your body, at least the *possibility* that this is true. In TI we talk about 'going to the place (in yourself) where the statement is true'.

An example of this for the professional actor might be the question of whether Hedda Gabler[9] is in love with Eilert – a question which has doubtless been asked by many actors who have taken on the role. But there is no certain answer to this question, and it is futile to try and build such firm answers into the given circumstances of the play. The whole concept of being in love or not being in love as absolutist notions is of little use to the actor, and in itself it solves no mysteries. Any female actor attempting this role needs to visit, in rehearsal, the *possibility* of being in love with the male actor playing the part of Eilert, and to let herself imaginatively and emotionally connect with the idea, so that she can explore, within this fictional situation, what 'being in love' means, to *her* Hedda, with *this* Eilert. At other points in rehearsal she can perhaps 'visit the place' where she finds him irritating, arrogant and small-minded. There are many other possibilities which she can explore within her attitude to Eilert – she can find the place where he is her brother, her father, a part of herself, her child, her nemesis, her saviour, or whatever. None of these is exclusively true, and yet none of them is definitely false either, because at various points she may experience the truth of every one of these 'statements' and respond to that truth in the moment. But to explore each and every one of these will enable her to embrace the complexity of the relationship and to stop pursuing elusive absolute truths which are simply not there to be found.

To return to the TI exercise: there is little point in the individuals merely intoning empty words, and such deceptions would be immediately spotted by the group in any case. The important thing here is that the individual can find the truth of the statement not in her head or in some invented fiction, but *in the situation itself.*

Before the individual comes back into the room, the group scatters through the space, so what the individual sees on returning is what appears to be, not a unified or potentially hostile group, but a diverse series of people with whom the individual can deal either as a group or in a series of one-to-ones. The individual also has the freedom of the space, so that 'going to the place where the statement is true' can be a spatial as well as an emotional shift. The group spokesperson tells the individual what the statement is, but no further comment is made, nor reasons given. The tutor or group leader reminds the individual that the task is to deliver the statement truthfully, and suggests that she should choose one person in the group to make the statement to in the first instance. Whom, in other words, will it be easiest to say this to?

In this case the individual's statement is 'I don't give a shit about any of you', and she chooses to make it to someone she perhaps strongly suspects *does* have that attitude. However, at this stage the individual is not only reluctant to expose to the group the side of herself which acknowledges the statement, but reluctant to admit that it even exists. Her defensiveness is quite understandable, since in our society we have a habit of pinning people to their public statements, even if those statements were made twenty years before in entirely different circumstances. In private we may say what we like, but in public we are taught to be careful what we say, to find one truth which is socially acceptable and adopt it as our absolute. In this case the everyday culture of the group demands that each individual demonstrates 'care' for every other individual. On one level this is quite reasonable, and conducive to building the 'trust' which is always so emphasised within acting groups. Within the space, however, that 'trust' has to extend further. You, the individuals within the group, have to trust each other enough to acknowledge the darker statements and less palatable truths which lie beneath the smiles, trusting that the basic transaction of mutual co-operation will still remain at the end of all this.

When working with acting groups which claim to 'trust' one another I always challenge them to define what they mean by that; to decide, in other words, how far that trust would extend. When we get down to the detail, unfortunately, it turns out that the trust is extremely limited. In many cases the actors are not able to trust each other even to be entirely reliable on the course, let alone outside class. Yet few are prepared to challenge the assumption of trust, or to analyse the nature of this transaction.

In this exercise we are attempting to rewrite the transaction which most groups set up with each group member from the start. The original transaction looks something like this:

We agree not to draw attention to your selfishness, egotism and contempt for the group, but instead to focus on your generosity, sympathy and respect	In return you agree not to draw attention to our selfishness, and egotism and contempt for the group, but instead to focus on our generosity, sympathy and respect

The new transaction is much more risky, and looks more like this:

We will allow you, in the acting space, to explore your darkest and most negative attitudes towards the group and individuals within it, in the search for a deeper knowledge of yourself and permission to express all sides of yourself	In return you will allow us, in the acting space, to explore our darkest and most negative attitudes towards the group and individuals within it, in the search for a deeper knowledge of ourselves and permission to express all sides of ourselves

The rewriting of this transaction – which relates *only* to work within the acting space – is risky because within that space, as in the outside world, there are consequences to every action and to every statement, which cannot be ignored or avoided. The new transaction states that the group will *allow* the expression of (possibly) negative or explosive statements by individuals, but that permission does not mean that at the time a statement is made the group will remain coolly detached from a statement or its implications. What it means is that *outside* the space the group will acknowledge that permission was given for the statement to be made, and that therefore in the outside world there should be no disapproval meted out to the individual who made the statement.

The upshot of this is that the individual within this exercise, faced with the statement 'I don't give a shit about any of you' will, once she has uttered the statement truthfully, have to face up to the impact the statement has upon the group and to the reactions she may get. The group has, after all, chosen the statement for her because they strongly suspect she is concealing from them feelings of contempt and indifference.

> The individual is now allowed to make her statement to anyone she selects within the group. She may decide to say it to someone who she suspects also feels that way, or she may be braver and choose the person she cares least for in the room in order to find the truth of the statement. Each person to whom she makes the statement comments on what they see, using the prefix 'I see someone who...' The individual then uses these reactions to help her make the statement again in a different way.

In the event, even when speaking to her chosen group member, the individual has tremendous difficulty connecting to the statement. She is very aware of the potential judgement of the group, and has convinced herself that the statement is untrue. In other words she is not even admitting that there was anything there to expose, let alone actually exposing it.

The statement, however, has to be made, and it is made, or at least the words of the statement are spoken. Immediately the group becomes aware that the individual is 'faking', making a statement which she neither believes in nor wants to have associated with her. The first group member to whom the statement is made challenges the individual, not by saying 'I don't believe you', which to some extent is what the individual wants to hear, but by saying 'you don't believe that'. The individual then has to take responsibility for disrespecting the group and for offering the statement in a way which is clearly disconnected and untruthful.

The individual is then caught between two places, neither of which she likes. She will either have to expose her lack of care for the group and risk the consequences of that, or expose her dishonesty and disrespect for the demands of the group within the exercise. In the event, she tries a third way, attempting through a raised voice and melodramatic gestures to convince the group that she believes in the statement. It is clear she is prepared for them to believe the statement on an intellectual level, but is terrified of letting either them or herself experience this on a visceral or emotional level.

From this point, the actor begins to work in a way which could be described as 'extremity acting'. This is a common strategy with actors who shy away from the reality of what they are doing. It involves a lot of strained facial expression, hand gestures and unsupported vocal gymnastics. Within this transaction the offer is something like: *'I want you to accept this statement, but I can't offer my own belief in it, so please accept all this arm-waving instead as a token of my sincerity.'* The response to this kind of offer may vary, but it could be along the lines of: *'I don't really accept your statement, but I want you to stop arm-waving because it's getting on my nerves, and I will offer you an acceptance which is equal in value to your belief.'* In this exercise, however, the group has demanded that the individual make the statement truthfully, and the response is much harsher: *'We don't accept the statement; you are faking and making us increasingly angry with your dishonesty.'*

Because the group is spaced out randomly round the room rather than sitting or standing as a single entity, the individual is able to take advantage of 'one-to-one' relationships, and to choose relationships within which she feels able to make the statement. At this point, however, her mind is still focused on the idea of convincing the group rather than on allowing them to see that part of her which makes the statement true. The group perceives that it is being treated to a series of manipulations rather than to a truthful statement, and the responses which the individual receives become increasingly contemptuous and angry.

That anger is then mirrored in the individual, who is annoyed by the responses she has received and by the accusation of dishonesty. She is also worried about her apparent inability to manipulate the mood of the group. Having found anger the individual is then able to make the statement with what seems like a truthful emotion, but the nature of the emotion itself is defensive and contradictory to the statement. In other words, by showing that the group can affect her emotionally, she has already shown the statement to be at least on one level untrue, and the group points this out. '*You clearly do give a shit*', is now the reply. The individual recognises what they are seeing and is baffled.

What happens eventually is that quite spontaneously the individual, having been rejected and mocked for her dishonesty by most if not all group members, and having passed through defensiveness, anger and frustration herself, loses her desire to please the group, and from that moment is able to offer the statement with perfect calm, clarity and sincerity. Within the parameters of the situation she has found a context for the statement and allowed herself to identify and expose that part of herself which quite genuinely does not care about the other group members – in other words, her egocentric part which puts herself first. The moment that she is able to make the statement with nothing but a sense of calm conviction is the moment when she realises the group is not offering her anything she wants or can accept. Paradoxically it is in the moment she gives up on them that she *can* give them what they want, and they can both recognise and accept it.

Once again, what this actor learns, or rather *experiences*, is that most situations within the space can offer actors the permission and context they need to make the statement which the text (or subtext) demands they make. In almost every case the dynamic of the space will lead the actor to a place where they can offer the statement as a truth within that moment, although its precise meaning in that context may come as a surprise.

The actor whose statement is 'I have no talent' has a similar experience, because his inability to commit to this statement is taken by the group as the clearest indication possible that the statement is true. Eventually this individual is faced with the universal opinion that he has no talent *because* he cannot allow us to see the part of him which believes he has no talent (and it's there in all of us!). Therefore in this moment, in this context, he has no talent. The moment this individual recognises and accepts this truth for what it is – the truth of *this* situation only, he can make the statement truthfully, and in that same moment, paradoxically it ceases to be true.

This may all sound very Zen, but it is all part of Transactional Improvisation's insistence that you find the truth of the moment *in* the moment, after which that truth may change and become something else. If you work from a fixed set of beliefs, either about yourself or about the character you are playing, you will be very closed to such possibilities. It is your job always to accept and explore, never to reject and deny.

5

Transactional Improvisation – Part Two

In the last chapter we started to look at the way in which the actor uses the group to create and make use of genuine human situations, which because they are real can be understood and responded to as such, without using tricks or forcing emotions. If we look back at the 'what-I-am' and the 'what-I-know' exercises described in that chapter, we might say the first exercise uses statements about *how the individual wants the group to perceive him*, while the second uses statements about *how the group wants the individual to perceive himself*. This chapter, by contrast, deals with statements illustrating *how the group perceives the individual*.

This is not about bringing personal agendas into the space, however, and as a group of actors you need to be clear about your professional discipline on that matter. Of course there is no way the group can pretend that it does not have knowledge of the individual as a person outside the space, but in TI you need to respect the privacy of the individual outside the training, and use only knowledge the whole group can recognise and relate to.

TI Exercise 3   The 'What-I-Do' Game

This game starts with the group working in pairs and observing their partner closely over a short period of time. You may notice many things about your partner, but you need to concentrate, not on fixed things, like blue eyes, big ears, or whatever, but on the way in which she presents herself. This may include choices she has made regarding clothing, hair, nails, etc, but it can also include her attitude, way of looking at you, signals she communicates either consciously or unconsciously, mannerisms and habits.

The tutor then calls everyone back together and picks on one person at random, asking him to make one observation about his partner, picking out a single aspect of their behaviour or presentation which could be judged or criticised by the group. In this case his partner is female and the observation is that she is flirtatious.

As in the previous exercise, the group now 'foregrounds' this issue so that it becomes for the moment of paramount importance. The observation also now becomes an accusation, and the accused becomes the offender. The offender is placed in the centre of the space, and each individual within the group considers and expresses why the identified quality is an offence to their group and society. The rules of the game state that an offence to one is an offence to all, so anyone who expresses a grievance against the individual is immediately supported by the group.

Individual women within the group quickly identify that they feel intimidated and belittled by this flirtatiousness. They feel the offender is seeking unfair advantage, mostly with the males, but with some females too. Several of the men, on the other hand, feel manipulated and disrespected. Others feel they are in some way having their worth judged. Both women and men feel angered by the dishonesty they perceive in flirtation. The group pushes the act of foregrounding quite far, and makes the offender feel very much the pariah, as the spirit of judgement and condemnation spreads through the space.

The individual is astonished, and at first inclined to be defensive at this judgement on what is to her a mere habit or personality trait. Her first impulse is to stick two fingers up and leave the space, and this option is left open to her. At the same time, however, it is pointed out that the aim of the exercise is for her to deal with the situation and secure her re-acceptance into the social group. To absent herself is a symbolic death in terms of the world that has been created by the exercise. In the event she stays in the space and begins to try and deal with her situation. Her strategies are made through her own choice, and could take many directions. On one occasion that this game was played, when *flirtatiousness* was indeed the charge, events proceeded as follows:

a Denial The individual pleaded innocence and asked the group to accept this. What the group actually saw, however, was her manipulation and dishonesty. One person commented that she was flirting at that very moment to try and gain acceptance. They rejected her offer out of hand, not least because to accept it would have exposed their own error in making the judgement in the first place. The individual didn't have enough belief in her own innocence to make the offer bigger, so she had to try a different approach.

b False confession She confessed to flirtatiousness and apologised. Once again, however, the group saw manipulation and more flirtation. They could see no remorse or belief in her own guilt, or recognition of its effect on the group. They pointed out to her that the more she made offers of this kind the more she was compounding the offence, because she was showing so little respect for their intelligence.

c Anger At this point the individual became genuinely angry. She resented the group's judgement of her, and became very defensive, questioning their right to challenge her. The breakthrough, in actor terms, is that she now at least believed in the genuineness of the situation, even if she was challenging its legitimacy. She had abandoned her first line of defence, which was to question the reality of the situation. The group responded to her anger with cold implacability, stating its demand with increasing conviction. The group was aware that the conscious manipulation had stopped, but also recognised that the individual had failed to offer her awareness of the offence, or the respect they demanded as her judges.

d Distress The individual's anger gave way to another emotion. The group was moved by it, and certain people began to waver in their determination to pursue the cause, but for the group as a whole the depth of emotion did not wipe away the offence, partly because the emotion was still defensive, and carried no admission of guilt, only the feeling of being perse- cuted. However, the group was now able to be gentler, taking an almost parental stance in explaining to the individual the nature and consequences of her offence. They could not give in to her because to do so would still expose their initial 'wrongness' in bringing her to this point. In fact, the greater the distress, the greater the cost to the group in giving in, because that would have exposed them as oppressors. Occasionally, mem- bers of the group, feeling guilty at the individual's distress, tried to distance themselves from the group, blaming others for the situation and siding with the individual. The group dealt harshly with such defection, because they were not prepared to let anyone within the group evade responsibility for what the group was giving itself permission to do – in this case to exercise a very harsh and exacting judgement.

e Realisation Finally the individual gave in, not just to the reality of the situation, but to the fact there was for her no other reality. Her defensiveness was over- come by her desire for acceptance, and she recognised that in this context, to offer genuine submission was the only way out. The group's mix of anger and solicitude opened the way, and she finally gave them what they wanted.

At this point the group wanted to accept the individual back into their midst, but I then stopped the exercise and threw a question at them. The individual may have paid her dues in terms of the original charge of flirtatiousness, but what about her obstinacy in refusing for such a long period to submit to their judgement? During that time she forced the group into the role of oppressor, potentially exposing them as cruel and unbending. The group has been abused, the transaction is not over, and the ball is in the individual's court.

> **f Openness**   For a brief moment the individual was puzzled, having thought she had paid her dues to her social group. She didn't, however, choose to return to defensiveness. Instead she studied the group to discover the extent of the abuse. For the first time she was genuinely observing them. Eventually she asked them to explain more fully what they wanted from her. The reply was that she had to discover it for herself. She was confused and a little resentful, but she knew she had to sacrifice that resentment, and did so, opening herself to the group and offering them the weakness which led to defensiveness in the first place. The group accepted her offer.

There is much more that could happen from there. The dynamic of the world does not stop, and it may be that at this point the group questions the actions and words of individual members, or even that certain members of the group still refuse to accept the individual. It is worth noting that this exercise has not required the individual to *lie* about him or herself, only to *reprioritise* the offence. The actor training issue here has nothing to do with the rights and wrongs of the issue itself, but with the following aspects of human transactional behaviour:

> 1 Acceptance that truth and morality are subjective, and socially/culturally defined. To a large extent we are what we are seen to be.

> 2 Awareness that the actor cannot bring the attitudes of their own world into the world of the play.

> 3 Discovery that submission can be a powerful tool in the cultural dynamic.

4 Understanding that the decision to change must connect to an emotional process of change in the body, otherwise the statement the actor makes will come across as false and manufactured.

The situation which the actor encountered here was actually a fictional one, and her first reaction was to stay firmly in her own world and *comment on* the fictional world from outside. In this case, however, the exercise demanded that she actually *enter* the world of the exercise, and deal with it from within. This required the actor to give up a certain amount of conscious control. One might describe this as 'getting rid of the director in the head', something all actors have to choose to do within the space.

On one occasion when performing this exercise, the actor who was being asked what he observed about his partner said she had a 'permanent scowl'. As it happened, no-one else in the group agreed with this, nor had they ever noticed this particular feature. They felt the observation was incorrect, and were unable to foreground an issue which they didn't believe existed. As a result, they spontaneously turned the accusation back on the astonished first actor, and made him face the charge of being a 'false accuser'. Faced with this charge, this actor was at first incredulous, refusing to accept even the validity of the group's decision, which he felt was 'breaking the rules' of the exercise. Eventually he had to accept that he could not singlehandedly support a reality which no-one else supported, and he gave in to the situation, if not to the charge.

The group then demanded a confession from him and a retraction of his initial statement. The actor had immense difficulty in fulfilling this demand. The internal struggle was palpable, and he fought so hard against it that, when eventually the demand became too much for him and he gave way, the shock of doing this brought tears into his eyes.

The 'what-you-do' exercise takes you towards the recognition that action in the space is conditioned by an understanding and acceptance of the given circumstances *in a dynamic relationship* with the interpersonal encounters in the space, and the task of the actor is to observe and buy into the events which take place. Most important choices in real life are made at a visceral as well as an intellectual level, and for the actor this must also be the case. Many actors, however, refuse to enter fully the world of the play, and even when they do allow their imaginations to take them there, many are also reluctant to give up control of that world, or to allow that world to change them internally. Yet without this simple act of submission, acting can never hope to mirror life, because it will always be limited by the boundaries of the individual conscious mind, rather than the boundaries of what is collectively possible through the mind and body.

The configuration of these processes might be drawn as follows:

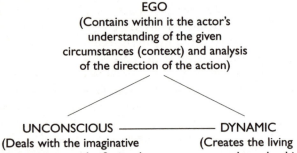

EGO
(Contains within it the actor's
understanding of the given
circumstances (context) and analysis
of the direction of the action)

UNCONSCIOUS ———————— **DYNAMIC**
(Deals with the imaginative   (Creates the living
commitment to the fictional   process through which
world and influences the actor's   ego and unconscious
emotional and physical choices)   negotiate)

It is not uncommon to see actors working on one or two of these levels, but ignoring the third. There are many performances which are very slick and controlled, and even responsive to other actors, but which have no emotional truth. Similarly there might be very truthful and responsive performances which jar because they don't seem to be operating within the given circumstances. Transactional Improvisation gets you used to the idea of confronting fictional situations as if they were real situations, for the simple reason that they *become* real in the moment. The question this inevitably raises is how do actors used to working as themselves within improvised situations then transfer these skills to the apparently more contrived world of scripted dialogue? The answer to this lies in the approach to rehearsal and performance, and the integration of improvisation into process, which this book deals with in later chapters.

6

Transactional Improvisation – Part Three

The next stage of Transactional Improvisation seeks to move you onto a plane of interaction in which you can experience even more fully the significance of *social context*. This stage takes into account not just the foregrounded issue and the immediate group dynamic, but also the ongoing process of 'conditioning' of the individual by the group. In other words, ultimately we do not have a discrete entity called 'the individual' interfacing with another discrete entity called 'the group', since each is at least partly created and shaped by the other. Identity, as you will discover, is largely a social construct, not an inborn quality.

Groups of training actors are no different from any other group, to the extent that after a relatively short time together, individuals within groups have a tendency to take on particular roles within the group which locate them within the group dynamic and 'pecking order.' One member of the group might become the 'joker' who makes others laugh and clowns around; another might become the 'counsellor' who listens to everyone's problems and offers advice and sympathy. Once these roles have been established, usually by the unspoken mutual consent of the individual and the group (though sometimes by the group alone) it is very hard to break free from them. Individuals (in their search for absolutes) find a security in fixed roles within the group dynamic which set parameters for their behaviours and responses to situations. To break out of a set role can be uncomfortable or scary, and may put one at risk of forfeiting the acceptance of the group.

Within, say, an office environment, such roles would exist largely without comment or challenge, and unless they became oppressive or discriminatory would probably assist rather than hinder the smooth running of the work. Wherever people are working together in groups to achieve specific objectives, the acceptance by each individual of his or her role within that process, and the broad acceptance by the group of each individual's position and contribution, are often essential to a successful outcome. In some cases the 'permissions' of an individual's role might be fairly broad; in other cases narrow. This depends largely on the nature of the environment and group objectives.

Within a group of actors, however, there is a dimension which could make such role-assigning problematic or even highly detrimental to the process. This is the fact that superimposed upon the 'real' world of the group is a series of fictional worlds, starting with the TI exercises which use that same group dynamic as a starting point, and ending with the most distant of fictional worlds offered to us by plays from other eras and cultures. Essential to the actor is the permission to inhabit different roles, in different worlds, without risking rejection by the group. An example might be a male actor whose 'sexual attractiveness' status in the group (for whatever reason) is low, being asked to play the part of a seducer. If the group refuses to give him permission to play the role, he will be faced, even when working on a text in an entirely fictional situation, with the limitations of his actual role within the group. If he is aware, as an actor must be, of the responses he is evoking in his fellow actors, he will have to confront the impossibility of ever achieving the character's aims, which may make it impossible for him successfully to play that part.

What can you do in this situation? An experienced actor might find enough conviction in himself to challenge and break out of the limitations imposed by the group. As an actor in training you are unlikely to have that kind of self-confidence. If you do not completely 'bottle out' of the role, you are likely to try and shut out the responses of the other actors, creating a performance in a bubble that looks and sounds completely disconnected from anyone else. In terms of your training you will have taken a step backwards in the process of trusting yourself and your fellow actors in the space, and you will be as stuck in your role within the group as ever.

I once directed an actor in the role of Baal in Brecht's play of that name. This actor had low status within the 'sexual pecking order', and during the early rehearsals became very upset and defensive that the reactions of the female actors to whom he was supposed to be irresistible were closer to amusement and contempt than sexual attraction. He challenged the female actors, who stated quite truthfully that *he* didn't believe in his appeal, so neither could they.

Eventually this actor realised that because Baal revels in his own ugliness and repulsiveness, challenging both the women's expectations of themselves and their sexual preferences, he could reach this character not by *breaking out* of his role within the group, but by *exploring* it to the full. The moment he began to accept and to play with his own ugliness, the miracle happened! The female actors began to respond to him. At first they were puzzled by this: 'I don't know what it is ... he disgusts me ... and yet there's something ... ' However, because the actor now believed in what he was doing, they had to as well, and so he broke out not by fighting and ranting against the group, but by submitting to their judgement. He had stopped trying to be the 'seducer' and allowed himself to be 'the hideous monster' in order to find what he needed.

This kind of 'super-acceptance' allows you to go with the flow, not against it. The mistake that many actors in training make is either to ignore the context within which rehearsals take place (which is of course once again the dynamic between the individual and the group) or to try and fight it. Neither works. The only thing that works is exploring the context as you find it and starting from there. A female actor whose role within the group is, say, 'the feminist' does not have to kill anything in herself in order to play Alison in *Look Back in Anger*. If she tries then she will end up doing a 'gritted teeth' performance in which part of her is constantly wanting to take the character in a different direction. She will never embody this role, she will only comment on it.

For this reason the actor playing Alison cannot and must not crush her beliefs and pretend to be someone she herself would disapprove of. Instead she has to use who she is, both in her own eyes and those of the group, to find a way into the role. What she might do in this instance is to put aside for the moment the political aspects of her feminism, and go back to the essence of what took her down that road in the first place – her awareness of injustice, possibly her anger and frustration, and her hunger for a life-situation in which she can feel respected and fulfilled as a woman (I suggest these only as possibilities). By returning to the basic problems and the emotional energy of those problems she can then start to work within the given circumstances of the play and experience the 'brick walls' which Alison constantly crashes against. Her journey will be complex and difficult, but within the circumstances of the play she will understand the choices the character makes because they will ultimately be her own choices. For Alison, at that time and in that place, there are no magic solutions and no political movements or feminist discourses to which she can turn. That is her experience, and if she is forced to channel her needs into her relationship with Jimmy, rather than into feminist action, then that is because within her circumstances she can see no other option.

This process of submission to one's own identity within the group is essential within the dynamic of a group of actors, and the next exercise is about how a group can *use* rather than oppose its own system of role-allocation, thus following the actor's rule that *the character you discover will not be someone else, it will be you in different circumstances.*

TI Exercise 4   Group Repetition

The first thing the group does is to assign each individual, with his or her consent, a role which is based on their experience of him or her within the group's social order. That role is summed up through a simple noun rather than an adjective – e.g. 'I am the mother', 'I am the truthteller', 'I am the rebel', 'I am the clown'. The group suggests the role and the individual endorses the choice (although it can work equally well the other way round). It should be

[63]

stressed that the choice of role is based on observation of what is, not what either the individual or the group would like to be the case.

Once the role has been assigned, each individual is caught within the confines of that role. The mother cannot relate to anyone in the group except on that level, although within this there are still many choices. The truthteller cannot lie, conceal or mitigate; the rebel cannot conform; the clown cannot 'fit in'.

Group Repetition is based loosely on the Meisner techniques dealt with in Chapters 7 and 8, although it is not in itself a Meisner exercise.

The tone, atmosphere and movement dynamic of the exercise should be akin to that of a party game, with everyone in the group using the space and spatial relationships to explore the 'permissions' of the game.

One person in the group volunteers to be 'the individual' and separates herself from the rest, announcing 'I am (e.g.) the mother.' The rest of the group (working outside their specific roles) then in unison repeats back to her 'You are the mother', responding to her physically and vocally in that role.

As with most repetition exercises this phrase can be repeated back and forth a few times, until the 'mother', observing what the group is doing, changes the comment to (for example) 'you're trying to hold my hand', upon which the group respond 'we're trying to hold your hand.' This comment also gets repeated back and forth, until either the individual or a member of the group observes something new happening which they can comment on, and therefore changes the comment again. This may happen very quickly and very often, but every comment made must be repeated at least once. Anyone within the group can also jump in at the appropriate point and comment on something the 'mother' is doing – for instance, if she is pushing them away someone might comment 'you're rejecting us', forcing the mother to repeat 'I'm rejecting you'. Comments introduced by members of the group should always be spoken on behalf of the group rather than just about one group member.

There are two other rules to this game, both of which need to be rigorously enforced both by the group and by the tutor. The first is that the 'mother' or whoever, must always be working within the parameters of that role. She cannot refuse to be the mother, or walk away from the role, in the same way that a real mother can't. She may find herself being a bad mother at times, but she needs continually to return to the role, exploring its demands and permissions physically, vocally and emotionally, rather than avoiding them, and she needs to find strategies to stay within the role when it becomes difficult. If she does back away from being the 'mother' then the group will notice and comment upon her dereliction of duty.

Finally there is the rule that when a comment is made, such as 'you're rejecting us', the mother must not repeat the comment back in a way that challenges it, as in 'I'm rejecting you??!!' She has to accept the truth of the group's perception, even if she personally doesn't feel she has rejected them. By accepting that rejection is what they see and repeating the comment back as her own, she will discover another dimension to her role. In a similar way the group must accept what the mother says about them.

The game can be played with each member of the group in turn playing out their assigned role. What you can discover by playing a role to its limits is your own frailty within that role, or even the antithesis of that role within yourself. The realisation comes at the point where you know that you no longer want to play that role but are being forced by the circumstances of the game to play it more and more. Merely giving up the role, however, is too easy. In order to continue to play the role, you must purge yourself of everything that is getting in the way, and it is this purging which effects the real change in how you see yourself. Take the 'seducer' for instance: if he allows himself to push the role further and further, and if the group allows him to do it, so that men and women alike submit to his seductive charm, the seducer will ultimately be confronted with his own loneliness and isolation. Part of him will be crying out to be seen as something other than the seducer, but the rules of the game compel him to continue, not just going through the motions of seduction, but genuinely seeking to find what he needs *through* the process of seduction. The repetition ensures that the actor and the group never run out of text – there is always something to comment on.

This exercise gives actors experience of another aspect of TI, which is 'negation'.[10] The principle of negation is that in order to move away from something you first move towards it, or vice versa. The actor who wants to offer a part of himself other than that which he feels he has access to in this moment, does not fight what is there – he offers what he has to such an extent that eventually he finds something else. Above all, he stops apologising for the role he plays within the group and commits to it absolutely.

I have often seen actors in despair at the huge difference between what they perceive happening before their eyes and what they feel should be happening within the rules of the improvisation or the given circumstances of the text. However, you only have to read Act 1 Scene 2 of *Richard III*, where Richard sets out to seduce Lady Anne, who hates him, to see how someone can turn one situation into something entirely different by making the right offers. Sometimes, however, it is hard to see this road, which is why the group repetition exercise described above is useful not just as an improvisation game, but as a way of exploring character. On one occasion I used it to help a female actor explore the role of Mary Warren in *The Crucible*. It rang particular bells for her, of course, because there is a section in Act 3 where Abigail and the girls *do* repeat everything she says. Initially the group gave Mary Warren the role of 'The Mouse', but when the exercise started she found it hard to play this role. The problem was that a mouse runs away from everything, and there is only so much running one can do before either being killed or escaping from the situation. The group revisited the text and found that before Mary Warren actually appears in Act 2 Elizabeth Proctor remarks about her: 'it is a mouse no more'. The group then decided to rename her as 'The Mongrel', meaning a sort of stray dog which seeks affection and protection from anyone who will give it, but is quite used to receiving kicks and beatings, and keeps going back for more. Her motivations are *fear* and *neediness*. Once the actress took on this role she had a totally different experience. Instead of running away from everyone she would constantly seek approval, shrinking back from blows but always returning to lick the face of her tormentor if offered even a little kindness.

When this actor returned to the text, she found herself in a different world. Instead of a rather one-dimensional fear and anxiety which she had previously tried so hard to maintain (not always successfully) from within, she now had a two-way transaction to work from. From this position she made better sense of the text, and of Mary's tendency to switch allegiance from moment to moment. Ultimately she found all her emotional life through the experience of being rejected rather than by forcing herself to express a fear she wasn't actually feeling. Once she had opened herself to rejection, of course, she found the fear easily without even trying.

What the actor can learn from this is that the role they choose to play either as themselves within a group or as a character within a play, must be transactional – in other words, it must be a role which gives them permission to establish an ongoing process of negotiation with the group. Actors choose their roles within the parameters set for them by the group – in other words, through their perception of the limits of their own status and social power. They must resist the temptation to play roles which by their very nature cut off negotiation and offer no possibility of change.

7

The World of the Play

Actors and directors often talk about the 'world' of the play. In Stanislavskian terms this might imply a sort of fictional universe, similar to our own but differing in certain key respects such as era, place and circumstances. The modern actor should perhaps not understand 'worlds' in such absolutist terms, but in the more subjective sense of the world of the individual. In other words, there are at least as many worlds as there are people, and each person sits at the centre of their own world. We do not live in the same world – we merely agree that certain features of our individual worlds appear to coincide. For instance, I may agree with the next person that a red traffic light means 'stop', but disagree that there is a God. There may be those who would argue that having a different view does not necessarily put us in a different world, but if we look at an extreme example, such as suicide bombers, we can see that the perceptual worlds inhabited by these people are not worlds which we can recognise. In fact, they are worlds which differ from our own in a number of fundamental respects, and the collision between these worlds and our own has been shown to be a lethal one. However, we need to remember one essential thing. Every action which an individual performs follows the internal logic of his individual world. We could argue there is no such thing as insanity – there is only what the individual perceives to be the truth. The schizophrenic who kills does so because in his very private world it is necessary to do so. The suicide bomber follows that path because she believes that she will receive salvation in an after-life. It is not for you, or anyone else, to say that one world is 'real' and another is 'make-believe'. You don't have to travel very far down that path to realise that reality is largely a matter of consensus. If everyone in the world suddenly decided that red was green then it would become so. Reality is also about power. In our society the media can decide what is beautiful and what is ugly, what is valuable and what is worthless, what is right and what is wrong, and to a large extent we accept their reality as our own.

Being an actor is about letting go of the idea that as 'sane' people we exist in the 'real' world, or that the worlds we have to enter as characters in a play are 'fictional'. To work from these assumptions is to keep one foot permanently in our own personal world in the mistaken belief that our personal world equates to a sort of central objective reality. If you are too secure within your own life, and consequently assume that reality is a fixed system of things, you will have difficulty letting go of that reality in favour of the world of the play. If, on the other hand, you accept your own perceptual reality is a selective and subjective amalgam of random pieces of information from which you struggle to assemble a coherent whole, you will have less difficulty stepping into an alternative world by means of reassembling some of those random pieces of information together with a few more pieces, which we call the 'given circumstances' of the play.

The rehearsal (and training) process facilitates this by allowing you to experience an alternative existence to your own, within the world of the plays. The more intense these experiences, the more real the world of the play can become, and the more it can stimulate real and spontaneous responses. In some cases the rehearsal experience can be such a prominent part of your life that it temporarily eclipses your everyday world, or begins to overlap with it. Up to a point this is no bad thing, although you need to be able to distinguish the parameters of the space from those outside, otherwise the 'permissions' of the world of the play can all too easily spill over into worlds where they are not appropriate. What you can accept, however, is that each time you truly and wholeheartedly venture into the world of a play, this too will form part of the totality of your life experience.

[69]

You may return to your own world, but to a greater or lesser extent the world of the play will have changed you irrevocably. An actor with many years' experience of many different roles must have come to accept that life is not linear and rooted in a single set of circumstances, but is a patchwork of different experiences, some of which are no less real for being located in the theatrical space.

In the training process we talk about you 'moving your centre' when you enter the world of an improvisation or a play. What this means in practical terms is that you work *within* the fictions of the world of the play, rather than standing outside and commenting on those fictions. Take for example Ibsen's *A Doll's House*. Very often when a group of actors read this play for the first time, the impression they get of Nora is of a weak and submissive person, while Torvald is seen as strong and oppressive, but this judgement is that of a twenty-first-century readership applying its own standards rather than those of the play. A closer reading reveals that Nora is anything but submissive – from the start of the play she is subverting and outwitting male authority, albeit within the narrow confines of her world. Conversely, Torvald shows himself from the very start to be timid and insecure, and is only able to exercise power by virtue of the patriarchal system he lives in. It is not just the characters' personalities which define their actions within the marriage, but the permissions and power structures of their worlds.

It may be true that for educated Europeans to conduct their marriage in this way in the twenty-first century would be shocking, but to judge Nora and Torvald's actions from the safety of our own worlds is utterly pointless. To be an actor you have to travel into these worlds and find out what they look like from within.

One of the temptations for the twenty-first-century actor when working on a play like *A Doll's House,* which is set in a more formal social environment than our own, is to *play* the formality rather than work to *subvert* the formality. This leads to very 'stiff' and stilted 'period acting' from which the audience concludes that no-one in that period was very expressive or interesting. This is rather like playing the boredom in Chekhov rather than trying to find a way out of it. Many late nineteenth-century plays are about people trapped in outdated social institutions and desperate to escape. The problem is that even their rebellions can seem pretty formal and conventional to us if we don't look beyond the rather stilted language. To discover the potential of these plays it is necessary to resist the temptation to associate the formality of the language with an equally formal and restricted acting style. It is essential that whatever the style of the language, the actors in Ibsen, or Chekhov, or Shakespeare, have experienced the world of the play in a way which makes them connect emotionally, mentally and physically with their character's situation, so they understand the choice of words from *within* that world, not from *outside*. In a well-written play the language is appropriate to the world of that play in a way that our personal language would not be, and you can use it to achieve your aims in situations where your own brand of verbal expression would prove inadequate.

Once you have really experienced what it feels like to exist in the world of the play, more than the language becomes accessible to you. Other permissions, such as movement and vocal choices, suggest themselves and become appropriate simply because you have imaginatively connected to the world of the play, and are working within it.

The first thing I would do with a group of actors working on *A Doll's House* (once we had read the play and researched the period) would be a series of improvisations which helped them to understand the parameters of this world and allowed them to pursue strategies within it rather than trying to play some externally perceived mood or atmospheric quality. At this point I would most probably ask the actors to work in quite formal rehearsal gear – long skirts for the women and collars and neckties for the men. A group of actors who have been used to working in tracksuits and trainers initially find these costumes constricting and awkward. What they soon notice, however, is the way the clothes affect their physicality and behaviour. However unfamiliar the clothes, there is a certain recognition in the body of the need to move, even to speak, differently. The problem is that their bodies haven't yet learned to be comfortable with this new physical demand, and at first they move stiffly and uncomfortably. It is important from the first to set tasks they can become immersed in, so they learn to work actively with and through the clothes, rather than letting the clothes impose upon them a formality which restricts their permissions. One such exercise runs as follows:

The 'Two Doors' Exercise

Two actors face each other in the middle of the space. The space has two exits. The actors can only leave the space together, but one wants to use Exit A, the other Exit B. The task of each actor is to persuade the other. Actor 1 may only use reasoned argument and verbal logic. Actor 2 may not use reasoned argument or logic, and is instructed to work mainly through physical offers and vocal sounds rather than words. Neither may use physical or verbal violence. Both must be prepared to submit if they run out of strategies. The aim is to win, but not by blocking the other person. However, it is better to lose than to reach stalemate. Both actors, but especially Actor 2, should experiment with physical as well as verbal strategies.

Very often Actor 1 is male and Actor 2 female, but this does not have to be the case, since it is useful for both sexes to explore both worlds. The direction this exercise can take varies tremendously, but it might go something like this: Actor 1 is confident and puts forward a good logical argument for leaving by Exit A. Actor 2 begins to launch into a logical counter-argument, but is reminded by the group that this is not an option. Initially she is confused and frustrated, and sometimes unable to find another strategy. She submits. Meanwhile the other actors in the group have been watching and they realise what is required. The next Actor 2 goes into child mode, manipulating Actor 1 with emotion, and sulks. She wins. The next Actor 1 is determined not to give in to such tricks, but this time Actor 2 is in temptress mode, blatantly using her sexuality. She wins. And so it goes on. Sometimes Actor 1 wins, sometimes Actor 2, but the outcome generally depends on how far each actor is prepared to go in pursuing the agenda. Successful manipulation requires Actor 2 to commit wholeheartedly to her offers, otherwise Actor 1 will see through them and crush them with logic.

Because each successive Actor 2 is trying something new and raising the stakes, Actor 1 has to raise them too, with the result that by the time the fourth or fifth pair is in the space, the two of them are as committed and determined as contestants in a boxing-ring. By the end, just by experiencing the conflict within these parameters, Actor 1 has found a level of authority and Actor 2 of emotional power which completely absorbs both of them. There is no question of standing outside the world of this exercise – there is only the inhabiting of the world and the battle to gain power within its walls.

As the actors lose their inhibitions and assume the full 'permissions' of the game, they also allow themselves to make fuller use of their bodies. When I have played this game with a series of couples, the physical gestures employed by each successive pair have become more and more extravagant. One female actor playing Actor 2 discovered a whole series of 'non-logical' strategies, of which the following are possible examples:

> **Collapse** – allowing herself to faint melodramatically into his arms or onto the floor, with the words 'I'll die if we don't go through that door!'
>
> **Seduction** – winding her body around his and tempting him, saying 'If you love me you'll come through that door with me!'
>
> **Liberation** – allowing herself to move freely and joyfully around the space like a child, saying 'You won't let me be free to go where I want!'
>
> **Tantrum** – falling into massive rages, flinging herself onto the floor or curling up in a ball, shouting 'I hate you, you're a horrible pig!'

By moving at will between these different gestures, this actor managed to keep Actor 1 constantly off balance, so that whatever physical attempts he made to impose authority on her, and whatever logical arguments he presented, she would always be able to shift the conflict onto a level where she had the upper hand. In this case Actor 1 also found gestures, some of which Actor 2 found hard to resist. These included:

Authority – a stern, upright body and sharp voice, plus phrases such as: 'You're being utterly childish, pull yourself together!'

Nurture – gentleness and caresses, together with a kind but firm tone, and phrases such as: 'You know I'm right, so you'll feel much better if you do what you're told.'

Briskness – a breezy untroubled manner, and phrases such as: 'Come on, we haven't time for all this nonsense!' or 'Dear dear, you're getting yourself into a state again!'

In this particular case Actor 2 won the battle, but she admitted afterwards there had been moments during the game where she was tempted to submit to Actor 1.

In the discussion which followed, the actors realised what they had done was to explore a simplified version of the worlds which Nora and Torvald inhabit. Asked if they found the worlds constricting or liberating, both Actor 1 and Actor 2 said they felt more liberated than constricted. This was not a political judgement, but a comment on the 'permissions' of the space. Many actors playing Actor 2, both male and female, remark that in their own worlds they don't feel they have permission to use those strategies, or at least not to that degree. Some of those playing Actor 1 also say that this behaviour in their own worlds would expose them to massive censure from their peers of both sexes. In exploring a restriction the actors realise they have also found a new set of permissions.

I once did this exercise with a female actor who although an excellent worker with a strong imagination found it extremely difficult to use the strategies which are open to Actor 2. She came from quite a tough industrial community where it was the norm to be as physically and vocally understated as possible. Hardness, toughness and monosyllables were her habitual mode. Being the creative and courageous person she was, however, she persevered until the point where she was able to employ all of the unfamiliar strategies described in the exercise, make them her own, and enjoy them. Afterwards she was both thrilled and shocked with herself. It was her first real experience of how far the permissions of other worlds can take you, even when that world may ultimately reveal itself as oppressive and hostile.

Improvisation is an essential tool of any actor, particularly one lacking experience, for finding and inhabiting strange worlds. The problem with much improvisation undertaken in rehearsal is that it doesn't set up clear parameters and agendas, and as a result can end up being vague and superficial. You should never be asked just to reproduce the surface appearance of the world of the play, even as a physical exercise. You always need to be working with the human desires and needs which lie beneath the surface. For instance, if I were to dress up my actors in evening dress and ball-gowns and get them to live in the world of a nineteenth century soirée, it would be essential for them to be working with the underlying agendas rather than with the external formality of the occasion. Sexuality, flirting, giving and receiving secret messages; power games, rivalries and sub-textual insults, these would be the stuff of the ballroom. The formalities, the kissed hands, the bows, the curtseys, the compliments, the dances, would merely be the parameters within which all this very visceral interaction could take place.

The 'Silent Signal' Exercise

This is a wordless improvisation in which men and women stroll around a room in formal dress, and on encountering each other first bow and curtsey, smile, and move on. After a while the man begins to observe the woman's physical and facial signals during each greeting, to see if she is offering a closer encounter. If he thinks he has read her signals correctly, he might proceed to take her hand and prolong eye contact. If this goes well and she seems to be giving more permission, he may even kiss her hand. However, if he has read wrongly and taken an unpardonable liberty, she shames him by hitting him with her fan. On the other hand, if he has read her invitation correctly the two of them may share a sensual moment or physical and eye contact before moving on. Despite the simplicity and relative restraint of this game, actors who have played it report that it is extraordinarily exciting trying to read signals

without words, and trying to have (or avoid) semi-sexual
encounters within a very public and formal arena.

It is necessary for you to discover what the world of the play
has to offer you. What part of you does it satisfy? What
permissions does it give which aren't normally available? If
you are a feminist in your own world then go and explore
being a docile housewife or a prostitute. If you are an atheist
go and explore being a Christian. If you are a communist go
and explore being a financier. We all have within us the
capacity, and sometimes even the urge, to be all things. You
need to work without guilt, and with immense enjoyment,
even if the flipside of that enjoyment is painful, as it will be
in most serious plays.

Entering the world of the play is ultimately about
permission. The group must give permission for each actor
to work truthfully and with commitment, even when doing
something which arouses distaste or contempt in the
spectator. You must give yourself permission to put aside
your own politics and morality and work within new
parameters – in other words, to move your centre.

MEASURING THE STAKES

If your life has been very 'cushioned' from violence, persecu-
tion, retribution or poverty, then you may find it hard to
appreciate imaginatively the extent of a character's need, the
risk she is taking by pursuing a course of action, and the
direness of the consequences should she fail. It is easy for the
tutor to remind you of how high the stakes are, but it is
perhaps harder for you to understand this if you have never
experienced vulnerability of that kind in your own life. The
questions 'how much does my character want this?' or 'what
will happen to my character should she fail to get this?' can
only be answered in the body and emotions – the intellect
alone cannot supply measures by which you can set your
responses.

There are few actors with a sufficient level of natural empathy and imagination to transport themselves physically and
emotionally into alien worlds without first having experienced

something akin to the character's situation. On the other hand it is clearly not possible to transport actors to war-zones or to situations of poverty and oppression as part of the rehearsal process. Many drama schools insist that their trainees have experiences outside their own comfortable and familiar worlds before starting their training, but even where you have previously put yourself in alien or uncomfortable situations, say through travel or voluntary work, there is no guarantee this will make you more able to connect with a fictional situation. Much will depend on how you have pro-cessed and understood your past experiences.

USING TRANSACTIONAL IMPROVISATION IN REHEARSAL

Transactional Improvisation exercises are one very useful way of allowing an actor to explore, if not the world of the play in a literal sense, then something very like it. The exercises described in Chapters 4-6 can be adapted to allow a company of actors to set up situations which mirror those in the world of the play not in every detail, but in some basic important aspects. To do this it is necessary to incorporate into the exercise some of the rules of the world of the play. In *A Doll's House*, for example, these rules say that a married woman may not make decisions independent of her husband. To be accepted both by her husband and by society at large she must submit to her role as willing assistant and decorative/sexual chattel. In return for this submission she (supposedly) receives protection and freedom from ultimate responsibility. This is the 'deal' which Nora apparently makes when she gets married, and it is this kind of transaction which the company can begin by exploring.

> We start with a repeat of the 'what-I-know' exercise described in Chapter 4. The company becomes society, and the actor playing Torvald is the leader of that society. The actor playing Nora is sent out of the room and while she is absent the company finds a statement which this particular female actor needs to make truthfully either about herself or about the company in order to gain acceptance within that society. Depending on the company's assessment of the actor, the statement might be anything from 'You're

clever and I'm stupid' to 'I'm weak and need your protection'
to 'I want you to tell me what to do'. Once the actor has
returned to the room and heard her statement, her task is
to make the statement in a way which gains acceptance.
She can use no other words.

Interestingly, it is not by looking inside herself for her own
submissiveness that she will gain that acceptance. Some
actors when given their statement choose to sit with
downcast eyes trying to 'psych' themselves into a place of
submission, but this in itself is an act of power and self-
control which is the opposite of submission, and the company spots this straight away. The point here is that you
cannot submit without having something to submit *to*;
therefore you can only understand the act of submission by
finding out precisely what the group wants from you and
giving it to them.

It may be that this actor, simply because she is a twenty-
first-century western woman, will find it hard to make her
statement without irony or disbelief. As she looks from one
company member to another she cannot bring herself to
believe that these people, or anyone else, could ask such a
thing of her in return for acceptance. The company, on the
other hand, is clear about its demand. The statement must be
made, and it must be made with truth and sincerity. More to
the point, the actor must find the reason for making the
statement within the people she makes it to. She must put
her trust in them.

Once again she is allowed to start by working with
individuals rather than the whole company. In this way she
can seek out the person she finds it easiest to make her statement to, and at the same time she can acknowledge that
society is not homogenous, but has potentially 'benign' and
'hostile' elements, which may have to be dealt with differently. If her statement is 'you're clever and I'm stupid' she
may be able to make that statement truthfully to one or two
people without much effort, but others will present her with
difficulties. Ultimately, though, she must make the statement
to everyone, and the responses she receives will reflect the
sincerity with which she has made it.

If the company, or one of its members, disbelieves her, they may challenge her verbally by stating, for example: 'I see someone who doesn't want to make this statement', or simply reject her by turning away. Company members who do believe and accept her statement may respond to her with a statement and a gesture which both offer acceptance and reinforce the paternalistic nature of the relationship. Hence they may stroke, soothe, tease or patronise her as they think fit, calling her a 'good, obedient, lovely girl', either to seal the relationship or possibly to test her submission.

These reactions can serve to remind the actor playing Nora that the deal she has signed up to with her society may expose her to a form of verbal and physical abuse which seems benign and caring but which will ultimately be dis-empowering or oppressive. This awareness may present another hurdle, since the actor must now make her statement again, from a different physical and emotional place which she may feel as an invasion of her person and sense of self. Still the statement must be made, and made sincerely. Whatever the situation the actor must find a reason to give in to it.

This is a great deal harder than it sounds, especially when it becomes clear to the actor that the company, in its role as the patriarchal society, is deliberately using its knowledge of her everyday persona within the group to place difficulties in her path and make submission difficult for her. When you are placed in this position you need to remain open and keep breathing without restriction to prevent tension occurring when the body's habitual defences spring into action.

Once the actor has succeeded in making the deal with the group on the benign and caring level which represents Nora's relationship with her father and her early time with Torvald, the company can begin to introduce more openly oppressive aspects into the transaction, possibly through their verbal responses, but certainly through the ways in which they demand physical submission from her.

The 'Do-It-My-Way' Exercise

This is an extension of the 'what-I-know' exercise. Once again the actor playing Nora has to make her statement to each member of the group, but now members of the group

can introduce oppressive elements, such as forcing her
continually to stand up and sit down, or making her walk
blindfold. These acts of oppression can be performed
without obvious violence or brutality which might in any
case make the actor simply shut down; on the contrary
they can be offered in an atmosphere of caring parental
love. Through all of it the actor must continue to work
towards submission and acceptance, still using her phrase
in each context to offer and justify that submission; if any
member of the company detects rebellion or anger in her,
the whole company will immediately withdraw all
acceptance and abandon her, and it will then be up to her
to find a way of rebuilding the relationship, still using only
her statement.

By gradually making it more and more difficult for the actor
to submit to them, the company pushes her towards rebellion. They may force her to dance for them, they may bom-
bard her with intrusive compliments, and although they will
never become openly cruel or hostile, they will make it more
and more difficult for her to keep submitting. If she has no
words other than her statement, it makes it even harder for
her to keep on being convincing, although she may be able to
turn this frustration into vulnerability.

Although some actors may be able to keep submitting to
the end, it is likely a point will be reached where they rebel,
though not in the easy confident way of the modern woman.
She will rebel because she has no other option – because she
has reached the end of her tolerance. Her rebellion takes
whatever form she wants it to, since by defying society she
also defies the exercise and all its rules. At this point the
group rejects her utterly and completely, and the first part of
the transaction is over.

There is an option here, however, for the actor playing
Torvald to break away from the rest and to try and get her to
find submission again, although her response in this case
may be unpredictable. For this actor too there may be
difficulties in understanding the world of the play. While he
may find it relatively easy to be paternalistic towards his
Nora, he will quite possibly not comprehend in its fullest
sense the need for a man to be, in the eyes of that society, in

absolute authority within his domestic life, and what it will do to his status and professional standing if this is seen not to be the case. Torvald articulates this fear at least once in the play, where he refuses to reinstate Krogstad simply *because* Nora has asked him to, fearing that society will assume his wife has control over him. Torvald's whole social existence, it would appear, depends on his ability to maintain his authority within the home.

Taking the exercise from the point where the actor playing Nora rebels, the group now sends the actor playing Torvald out of the room, and decides on a statement for him, which can be made both to Nora and to the group. This statement must be made in a way which both invites the rebellious (and excluded) Nora to accept his authority, and convinces the group that he is in control. His statement may vary, but it could be something like: 'There is complete harmony within my home.' While these are all the words he has, the actor playing Torvald can use whatever physical gestures he wants to, and this option is also open to the group members as they respond to his statement. What he has to bear in mind, however, is that it is not just the repair of the relationship he is pursuing, but the acceptance of his statement by society. The company can, if they feel he is losing, reject him too. His social acceptance depends on his physical and verbal ability to make the actor playing Nora accept his statement.

Working from this point in the exercise the actor playing Torvald may have a hard job turning around Nora's rebellion, and convincing the group of his authority. However, whether he succeeds or fails, what the actor will experience is his own struggle to regain control and also the contempt of society as they view his attempts to do so. In his efforts to subdue Nora, the actor may have to employ both hard and soft parental measures, and if these do not do the trick, his failure will be further exposed. It is possible, of course, that he may succeed in winning Nora back. If this happens, it may provide useful clues about the dynamic which these two actors may ultimately discover as they explore their relationship.

This is one example of a TI exercise which allows the actors to experience the world of the play within the world of the company and the space, simply by allowing the company to set new parameters for their relationship with the group. Having taken an exercise of this kind to its conclusion, the actor playing Nora will be in no doubt about the potential of the acting company to take on and enjoy this benignly oppressive behaviour. She may also have strong suspicions that it is only the different social rules and conditioning within the twenty-first century that stops some of them from behaving like that anyway and being allowed to do so. For this reason it is essential that actors do not perform an 'apology' ritual with each other, where after a difficult workshop they say 'sorry' to each other and have group hugs to try and distance themselves from the events of the session. What they need to understand is that trust within an acting company must be about acknowledging and accepting each other's darker potentials, not ignoring them or pretending they aren't real. With this understanding comes the recognition that plays are not about alien beings doing alien things, but that every facet of human behaviour ever written about is already within the scope of this company of actors and can happen within this space.

Once again, it is essential when improvising round a play you do not concern yourself just with externals and surface appearances. The world of *A Doll's House* is one thing for Torvald and something very different for Nora, although both may have their up-sides and down-sides for the actors concerned. More importantly, however, you need to realise that the worlds you inhabit in the space are not Henrik Ibsen's but your own. You discover these worlds by setting up improvisation situations where the 'social transaction' – the agreement whereby the individual buys into a set of social rules in return for acceptance, status and security – breaks down, simply because the gap between what is demanded and what is offered becomes too great. It is the first-hand experience of this breakdown, on a simple improvisational level, which will allow you to understand and inhabit the world of the play, and which will make the act of improvisation itself a transformative process. There is no need for you to travel across continents or go back in time to understand plays or characters – everything you need to explore the world of the play is already there with you in the space.

8

Approaches to Text – Part One

A key aspect of most acting work is the business of learning words written by someone else and delivering them in a way that sounds as though you have just thought them up on the spur of the moment. This is anything but a natural process, and many people who lack actor training find it next to impossible to speak words which are not their own in a way which either communicates meaning effectively or stimulates the ear to listen. Others, such as preachers, politicians or newsreaders, are trained to speak in a way which although very far from spontaneous human speech, uses patterns of breath and intonation which do make us listen, but render us passive and receptive rather than active and responsive.

One of the skills which we are probably all born with is the ability to detect emotional quality in the voices of others. Even before we understand actual words we respond to tone and are able on a very visceral level to identify how others feel about us. For most of us, the way we speak as adults is governed by a direct relationship between our understanding of the people and situations before us and our inner emotional state. If we consciously or unconsciously feel the need to suppress our inner emotions, this will normally be by constricting the free flow of breath in and out of our bodies, so the voice seems to sound in the head rather than in the body. The 'head voice' may still express emotion, but because it is not 'connected' to the body, the sound the other person hears will lack that deeper ring of truth. The words and gestures will suggest a level of emotion, but the resonance of the sound will not confirm that the emotion is actually present in the body. For the really aware listener this will serve as a warning bell that the speaker is not really sincere, or perhaps that there is more to this situation than the speaker is indicating.

Audience members occasionally find themselves left strangely unmoved by what should in theory be a deeply emotional scene. This may be puzzling, especially if it is clear that the actors are working hard and with energy. The most likely explanation for this is once again that the actors are not breathing properly, that their voices do not have that deeper support and connection to the moment which to the audience signals they are both affecting and being affected by each other.

Where there is no breath connection you will also often get 'falling inflexions', where the vocal pitch repeatedly descends in the same way on the last syllable or word of each phrase, closing down every statement instead of keeping the issue alive through upward or level inflexion. This is because actors with no breath connection find it hard to sustain the energy of the line, and often run out of breath, so they can't carry the thought or the emotion through to the end. The result is often a repetitive rhythmic pattern which not only lacks resonance but also alerts the listener to the artificiality of the vocal choices.

Many actors make the mistake of believing that the expression of emotion on stage is about contorted faces, strangled voices and arm-waving. To the audience, however, this comes across largely as sound and fury signifying nothing. Others may think that to dig into themselves for an emotion and then wash a scene with that emotion is truthful acting, but here all the audience will see is someone who is so stuck in an emotional swamp that nothing the other characters do can affect them. In either case the text will seem to be stuck, and will lack either vocal truth or responsiveness to a changing situation.

There are also the actors who have been trained to breathe and speak from their centre – and to that extent sound connected and truthful – but have rehearsed their words in such a way that each stress, each pitch change, each pace variation, is so predetermined that although the audience may begin by listening, they soon become aware they are experiencing something rehearsed. In other words, there is nothing actually *happening* in the scene, nothing is at stake, and the actors are merely reciting rather than playing to achieve anything. The audience may be impressed but will be strangely bored.

FINDING THE AGENDA

The only way to deliver text organically, as you would speak in real life, is to be *using* the text to achieve something in the situation which you and the other actors have set up. Once you have understood the given circumstances of the play, and have a clear idea of who the other characters are and where they stand in relation to you, you are in a good place to decide on your *agenda*. The agenda is similar to the Stanislavskian 'objective', the difference being that the objective is what the character apparently wants to achieve throughout the scene or unit, whereas the agenda is simply what the character came to the space to do.

An example from *A Doll's House* could be Mrs Linde's first meeting with Nora in Act 1. It is clear from the text that Mrs Linde's principal agenda at the start of this scene is to find work at the bank Torvald manages. However, if the actor playing Mrs Linde relentlessly pursues this one idea throughout the scene, then the relationship will appear very one-dimensional. The text indicates that Mrs Linde finds it hard to resist scolding Nora and pouring scorn on her endeavours, perhaps echoing their schoolgirl relationship, in a way which may well undermine her agenda rather than support it. Ultimately the scene becomes quite a complex process of readjustment, as the two women try and define their status with each other, and the agenda, while in this case still *present*, is often not *foregrounded* within the dialogue.

Depending on the text and the actors' relationship with each other, once the scene has started the agenda can remain the same, can strengthen, can alter slightly, can change completely, or whatever – it doesn't really matter. The agenda is merely the energy or impetus which pitches you into the space and ensures that you begin the scene with the right level of urgency. In real life you can get distracted momentarily even from the most urgent agenda – that doesn't matter, provided that at some point you come back to it. In drama the text will guide you back to the main issue, and if you trust it to do so you can allow yourself to notice and respond to what the other actors are doing along the way, without losing your way within the drama.

What happens once you are in the space is that a process of negotiation begins with the other actors, within the parameters of the text, the characters and the circumstances prescribed by the play and the actors' understanding of the play. The trick is to know your text and to know the background circumstances so absolutely that you don't have to think about them, nor do you have to force your imagination to create the world of the play – you merely allow all that you know of this world to exist in the space, allow the action to happen, and by speaking and hearing the text, steer the action in whatever direction the words seem to demand.

Stanislavski talks about the three inner motive forces of the actor, which he defines as *feeling, mind* and *will* – in other words, the actor's emotional empathy, analysis and individual drive. I would prefer to talk about *openness, intellect* and *courage.*

Openness is the permission to let the breath 'drop in' to the body without hindrance, creating an instant and organic connection between thought and emotion.

Intellect is the mental faculty which allows us to connect with the play on both a factual/ contextual/ historical level and on a personal/imaginative level.

Courage is the permission to play a scene like a poker game, not anticipating outcomes but observing and working to affect the other players, and using the text and the space as your cards.

If you are working with all three qualities you will have a profound understanding of the circumstances and journey of the play, a receptive mind and body, and what could almost be termed an addiction to the moment or the adrenalin of negotiating the moment. This is something which actors often describe as the 'buzz' they get from working.

OWNING THE TEXT

One thing which you must always remember about text is that with the possible exception of Shakespearean verse, text does not 'drive' the action. *You* drive the action by appearing in the space with a strong agenda and responding to what you find there. The text is merely a tool which in order to have meaning must have a *context.* Only when there is a clear and dynamic context in which you can move and speak will the text make any real sense, because if the audience cannot equate the messages which they are receiving from the actors' bodies, and from the tonal qualities of the voice, with the actual meaning of the words, they will be either bored or possibly confused and frustrated.

This all sounds very simple, but as every actor knows, finding one's way through certain texts and understanding how to use the words most effectively is not always an easy task. Densely written or archaic text, whose style is formal, aphoristic or didactic, may sit uncomfortably in the body of an actor who has been brought up with more casual mini-malistic forms of language, such as those used in text mes-saging or internet chatrooms. There is no easy way round this – nor is there any substitute for the lengthy though rewarding process of reading, interpreting and speaking unfamiliar forms of text over and over again until the actor gains full ownership of those words. The good news is that once you have gained mastery of one 'alien' style, the next one you try will be easier, and so on, until the process be-comes considerably shorter and less daunting. The point is, you must be able to fool the audience into thinking that you have spoken in this way all your life, and that this form of expression is entirely natural to you. This could mean two pages of politically discursive monologue within a Bernard Shaw play, or elaborately turned quick-fire wit within a Restoration piece.

To achieve this familiarity obviously requires the actor to study the text and to gain an understanding of the words, phrases, metaphors, images, references and witticisms. Next the actor has to practise articulating the words aloud so that the 'brain-to-mouth' relationship is in place. Experienced

actors may be able to articulate most sounds fairly immediately, but this is a skill honed over many years, and most
trainees will need extensive practice at it. Many actors when
practising their words use mental images to help them articulate more easily. For instance, if you are using the tongue-
twister 'a proper cup of coffee in a proper copper coffee pot',
you are far less likely to stumble if you can imagine the
copper coffee pot in question, so that the process is one of
describing something which already exists in your mind's eye
rather than merely intoning the sounds. In the same way,
when working on text, you need to visualise the words and
images so that the connection between word and thought
can begin.

You must also use the breath to take the words into the
body. This is not difficult provided you are letting the breath
drop into the body without hindrance. The sound of a word
can then resonate in the body and affect the body's impulses.
However, spoken words are not empty sounds. They have
meaning, thought and image – in other words, they *signify*.
There is also a relationship between sound and meaning
which when the word was first created probably emanated
from the body, which is why the sound of a word often
reflects its meaning. If you allow both the sound of a word
and its meaning in that context to affect the body through
the breath, in so doing you *connect* thought with emotion
and you allow this connection to express itself through the
voice and body.

These are some of the first steps which you can take towards *owning* the text. The play may have been written by
someone else, but by the time you speak the words in the
space the audience must be prepared to accept that you have
made them up on the spot. If we stop to think about it, very
little of what we say in our real lives is actually original. Most
of it consists of phrases and expressions which we have
picked up in their entirety from someone else and made our
own. If the ownership is incomplete then the phrase may
sound awkward and artificial in our mouths. This often happens when young children pick up and use phrases which they
have heard without being completely sure of their meaning.

It is the incongruity of the phrase in the mouth of a child which makes us laugh. When adults do it we are less inclined to laugh and more inclined to be embarrassed for them. When actors do it we should ask for our money back!

You need to have full ownership of the text, and the journey towards this point may involve a variety of different techniques and exercises, depending to a large extent on the type of text. Among the most crucial of these exercises are those which allow you to build an emotional connection with the text by associating what the text suggests the character may be doing, with transactional processes which you can recognise as your own.

ACTIONS VS. OFFERS

Those actors who have studied The System or trained using broadly Stanislavskian methods may be familiar with the concepts of *units* and *objectives*. Anyone who has gone further and worked with the later Stanislavskian technique of 'psycho-physical actioning' may also have used *action verbs* – transitive verbs applied to each line or phrase of text which apparently sum up what the character is doing through that line of text. Examples might be 'I patronise', 'I blame', 'I chastise', 'I threaten'. This is supposed to give the actor a psychological and physical sense of how to deliver the line.

The problem with these transitive verbs lies in the fact they only refer to the action itself, and not to the nature of the transaction. A verb is a 'doing' word, and a transitive verb describes an action which can be done to another person. However, the verb itself sets up no relationship between the actor and the action, nor does it provide a context within which the action can take place. In transactional terms it is devoid of meaning in the same way that the verbs 'I sell to' or 'I buy from' are meaningless unless we know what is sold, what is bought, and how much is paid in each case!

Actors who use psycho-physical actioning may be clear what the nature of the action is, and may be playing that action with impressive energy, but unless their offers are taking place within a clear transactional context, the verbs which bat back and forth will not connect with each other, and the whole scene will descend into a series of one-person shows which happen to be taking place in the same space.

A transactional actor views text, not as a series of actions, but as a series of *offers* and *counter-offers*. In Chapter 3 we looked at how offers work within real life and in improvisation situations. Now we can also apply them to text. The difference between an *action* (in the Stanislavskian sense) and an *offer* is that an offer demands to be accepted, and for something to be given in return. Similarly, if you receive an offer, and are able to read the nature of the offer and the demand which accompanies it, it is hard to ignore. There is an emotional as well as a literal content, which you can respond to viscerally as well as intellectually. In other words, to make someone an offer is to engage their full attention, mind and body, because if they identify that an offer has been made, they won't be able to resist considering it – of such stuff are human beings made!

Transactional acting begins with the assumption that most if not all dramatic scenes can be deconstructed thus: Actor 1 makes an offer, perhaps the offer which starts the scene. Actor 2 notes this offer, but at this stage rarely either accepts or rejects it. A dramatic scene by definition revolves around conflict, and the journey of the scene will usually be about the attempt to resolve that conflict, either through agreement or by the defeat of one party by the other. For Actor 2 either to accept the offer or to reject it outright means in effect the end of the scene, the end of the journey. From that point there will be nothing for the audience to watch, nothing for the actors to play for. What Actor 2 will almost certainly do instead is to *counter-offer* – to make an offer which deflects the attention of Actor 1 away from the urgency of the first offer and onto something else, which is a form of rejection, but which still leaves the door open to further negotiation. Actor 1 may see the counter-offer, but in most cases refuses to be deflected, and counter-offers back, either through a reiteration of the first offer (only more so) or through a new offer.

In Act 1 Scene 7 of *Macbeth* there is a good example of this kind of transaction, as Macbeth and Lady Macbeth offer and counter-offer in order to resolve the issue of whether or not to murder King Duncan and usurp his throne.

Macbeth's first speech of the scene begins with the line:

We will proceed no further in this business

The precise nature of this offer will be up to the actor, but it could be *authority* (as her husband), or it could be *fear*, or it could be *loyalty* (to the King). In each case the demand is for *compliance* with his decision. Whatever the offer, the circumstances dictate that Lady Macbeth cannot afford to reject his offer outright, since this will inevitably mean that he will go his own way leaving her powerless. Nor can she afford to accept his offer and dash all her own hopes.

What she does is to counter-offer with *contempt*, in the speech beginning:

Was the hope drunk,
Wherein you dress'd yourself? Hath it slept since?
And wakes it now to look so green and pale
At what it did so freely. From this time
Such I account thy love.

Macbeth clearly sees the contempt, and the accompanying demand for *manliness*, so he counter-offers with *caution*, or possibly *common sense:*

I dare do all that may become a man:
Who dares do more, is none.

She comes back with *contempt* again, but with the stakes raised, and then strengthens this offer with further offers, possibly of *belief* (in him) and *ruthlessness*. In other words she realises that just to belittle him may drive him away, and so she both sweetens the contempt and sets herself up as something for him to match. Macbeth is still not able to accept her offer, nor fulfil her demand, and he now makes the mistake of offering her his *fear* or *apprehension:*

If we should fail?

This she quickly counters with *confidence* and *resolve:*

But screw your courage to the sticking-place,
And we'll not fail.

Macbeth's response is to offer *admiration* and *confidence* (in her), demanding her *leadership* and *optimism*, which she freely supplies, while at the same time demanding his *compliance*. *I am settled* says Macbeth, finally *accepting* and thereby ending the scene.

The series of offers which you choose are based on a discussion of what the demands of the text appear to be. Within reason they are open to interpretation, but it is usually best to start with the obvious. Making the wrong offer not only feels wrong, but it can often muddy the text. Making the right offer almost always feels right, and enables you to deliver the lines with clarity.

You do not have to restrict yourself to one offer per speech, either. In a longer speech you may clearly decide to change the offer or to top one offer with something else. Once again the choice of offer is dictated by your interpretation of the text, but the strength and the manner of each offer will be influenced by the other actors, and how they appear to be reacting. As in real life, if you are making an offer to someone, it is the way they react which prompts you either to make the offer differently or to change to a different offer. Thus if Macbeth turns away from his wife and tries to ignore her, she will have to respond physically and vocally in a way which takes this into account. If on the other hand he sits down and looks shaky and ill, a different version of the same offer will be necessary.

Those who agree with David Mamet[11] might feel that actors should have no need for these offers – that a truthful response in the moment will automatically bring out the right level of offer without needing to define it beforehand. The reality is that, especially when working with complex and heightened text, most actors find a liberation and a permission in the notion of a personal offer. What the offer does is to give the actor ownership of the *context*, from which he can quickly progress to ownership of the *text*.

THE OFFER CONVERSATION

One way of establishing this ownership is initially to put the text to one side, and let the actors move freely within the space having an 'offer conversation'. Prior to the offer conversation the actors work out the offers which the text suggests, and then start to play the shape of the scene, replacing the text with the statements of the offers, so the actor actually *says* 'I offer you my authority' (or whatever), matching the physicality and the vocality of the offer to the word. The phrase can be repeated, changing according to the physical response it gets, until the other actor is ready to come back with her offer. Both actors and observers are keenly aware that the offers have to be what they say they are. If the physical and vocal dimensions of the offer do not seem to fit the words then the group can challenge the actor to make the offer differently.

As with all transactional work, you do not have to search inside yourself for the emotional energy to make the offer – you can find it in the other person. The more you try to evade the offer, the stronger and more insistent it will need to become. The offer conversation gives you the opportunity to build the energy of the scene by sparking off one another, and to explore the variety of ways in which offers can be made.

Offer conversations are particularly useful for moving you out of habitual physical and vocal pathways. Because the offers have been decided upon beforehand, and because the rules of the offer conversation state that all offers must be clear and strong, you will be constantly faced with having to make new choices and to go in different directions. If your scene partner has been winding you up by offering *arrogance* then your habitual response might be to offer *anger*, but your stated offer, in the context of the play, could be *meekness*. Your job within the offer conversation is to find a reason in the moment to offer *meekness* and not *anger*. By making a different choice you can explore a new pathway without sacrificing ownership of the scene.

At this point I can hear you referring me indignantly back to my earlier criticism of Stanislavski in which the idea of the actor 'mapping' a scene was dismissed as prescriptive and artificial. What needs to be made clear about these offers is that they are only springboards for exploration, used in the earlier stages of rehearsal. They serve to focus your mind on the demands of the text and help to bridge the 'unfamiliarity gap' between what the author appears to be suggesting and your own physical/emotional life. What the offers should never do is pull you out of the moment or stop you looking at what is happening in the space. If it is genuinely impossible for you to find a way of making the chosen offer in the actual context of the space, then the offer may have to be changed. The other point which needs to be made here is that the offers which you have chosen are not the only offers you will make in the space; they are merely the main ones suggested by the text. You will make many others without even realising, and this is as it should be.

Having said that, as I mentioned in Chapter 2, many new actors confuse their own habitual responses to situations with 'natural' reactions. 'I can't do that – it doesn't feel natural!' they complain. The reality is that our responses to every situation in our lives are shaped by the conditioning forces which we recognise and work within as our parameters. The choices we make in each moment are based on that awareness, and although these may not be reasoned or intellectual choices, they could still have gone another way had the circumstances been even slightly different.

When you are working in the theatrical space, removed from your personal realities, you may have an unfortunate tendency to use even fewer choices and pathways than you would in your own life. The awareness and self-consciousness of 'being an actor' may push you into a series of 'theatrical' choices which often fail to reflect either the demands of the text or the reality of the moment. These habitual and disconnected responses are often characterised by body tension, forced vocality and blocked energy, and the experience for the audience is of trapped emotion, which you are unable to release into the space. On a purely technical level this is because you are trying to work from your head rather than your body, and consequently are forgetting to *breathe*.

You do not have to justify your choices to yourself or to anyone else in the moment; you only have to *breathe* and *do*.

Breath and openness are the most important factors for maintaining the truthfulness and dynamic of any dramatic scene. If you have to make a counter-offer which requires you to re-channel your energy, then it is through the breath that this will happen. The reason for changing and the permission to change are found in the other actors; the process by which that change is allowed to happen at an emotional level is dependent on the breath. Chapter 11 of this book deals with Voice and Movement, and how you can learn to find and maintain the necessary openness.

Another useful aspect of offer conversations is that they instantly call for physical activity and energy, which can ultimately be channelled back through the text. It is essential for offer conversations to take place in dynamic contexts which in some measure reflect the inner condition of the character outwards into the space. For instance, an offer conversation based on the above scene from *Macbeth* could be played out using other members of the group to create atmosphere, as follows:

Offer Conversations in the Space

The group spreads out through the space and forms a series of individual frozen statues, like a grotesque waxworks museum. These might reflect the images of murder, or perhaps of power, which could be present in Macbeth's mind. The two principal actors in the scene use this 'body landscape' as a physical and spatial context for their offer conversation, moving freely around the space, and relating to the frozen bodies, in whatever way they want to in the moment, seeing them as shapes, as people or as metaphors and externalised images reflecting their own thoughts and emotions.

As in Grandmother's Footsteps, these statues can change shape, but only behind Macbeth's back, though he is constantly trying to catch them moving. For Macbeth the statues become the frightening aspects of his wife's personality or of his own darker nature which he cannot control. By contrast Lady Macbeth may have a sensual and tactile relationship with these human waxworks, making each offer statement refer to them, taunting Macbeth with the shapes and inviting him to touch them.

The physical and vocal choices you make in this space are entirely up to you, but because the exercise removes the scene from a conventional rehearsal/performance context, you will almost certainly find a freedom in that, and be able to explore this context without the debilitating self-consciousness which 'being an actor in rehearsal' can engender.

What you will usually find in this exercise is that the physical activity in the space and the words which you use to make the offers will be continually negotiating with each other. Sometimes the offer and the physical activity will be completely in tune with one another; at other times you will have to change the physical activity, or make the offer differently, in order to find that connection and retain the truth of both. In this example Macbeth by definition has less control over the ensemble and a different physical role in the space from that of Lady Macbeth, which means that the actor playing Macbeth has to do more 'ducking and diving', while she is able to shape and manipulate.

In one version of this exercise, the actor playing Macbeth was so harassed by the changing shapes in the ensemble that he had to find a place in the space from which he could no longer see them before he could bring himself to make the offer of 'common-sense', which meant that the offer, although sincere, was weak, and depended on his position over by the wall. By physically pulling him back into visual contact with the ensemble, Lady Macbeth was then able to use his reactions to fuel her offer of 'contempt'.

Once you have used the offer conversation a few times, you can start to use the text within the same physical exercise. The text is then fed into something which is already dynamic and over which you have ownership. The results can be startling. For actors who have been forced to work solely with the offer statements, suddenly to have the text with all its comparative richness of language available to them is revelatory. This is another example of the text *not* driving the action. *You* drive the action by being alive and wanting something from one another; the text is just one of the tools which you can use to get what you want. The text can help steer the action into one place or another, but it is not the driving force. Ownership of the text means that by creating the action you also create the need for the text, and therefore the right to speak it as an actor.

The 'Shaping' Exercise

This is another ensemble game which helps actors locate their text in a series of changing contexts. As in the previous exercise, the ensemble members scatter through the space and create individual tableaux with their bodies. The two principals in this case are working on a scene from *A Doll's House*. The first character in the scene to speak is Torvald, but before speaking a line he allows himself to explore the physical space and the shapes within it. He can move non-naturalistically, using different levels. Eventually he goes to one of the frozen figures, and slowly reshapes the statue into another form. The ensemble actor allows herself to be sculpted in this way. As the principal actor performs this action he speaks his first line of text. Once he has finished reshaping, he freezes, upon which the ensemble actor he has sculpted comes to life and performs the same action on him. Once the principal has himself been sculpted, he holds the position for a few moments, before moving on to another figure and repeating the process. Meanwhile his scene partner has been doing the same thing elsewhere in the space.

The whole scene is played out through this process of reshaping and being reshaped. The dialogue simply fits around the physical process, so that neither actor has any preconception about the physical context within which they will find themselves speaking any particular line. All they have to do is breathe, let themselves be affected by the situation, and to speak from within the total context, which will include their physical experience, their awareness of the whole space, and the aural stimulus of their scene partner's lines spoken from elsewhere in the space.

This exercise ensures that both principal actors experience how it feels to speak both from a position of physical dominance, and from one of physical submission, without being able to decide beforehand which lines of dialogue will be spoken from which position. The acts of sculpting and of submitting to being sculpted can be highly emotive experiences, which means this exercise provides you with a powerful physical context within which to make spontaneous choices about the text. It can also have the effect of slowing your delivery down and heightening the words of the text, while also encouraging breathing and reducing your body tension. In this way you can experience both the power and sensuality of the text, so that your words affect you as well as the other actor.

Using the ensemble within rehearsal makes a lot more sense than having ten or so actors sitting around the edge of the space waiting for their 'turn' in the middle. Actors who have watched their colleagues floundering through the early stages of 'moving' a scene quickly become bored and uninspired, and even the most keen and professional can lose energy, with a knock-on effect on the atmosphere and energy levels within the space. There are many more ways of usefully employing the group as an ensemble, to assist with the creation of atmosphere, to provide the principal actors with physical and spatial options within the space and a context within which they can explore. Chapters 9, 10, 14 and 15 of this book suggest further exercises which employ the ensemble in the exploration of text. In general terms, however, the ensemble can be used in two ways:

1   To create an atmosphere, through improvised sound and movement, which has a direct and visceral effect on the principal actors: The ensemble can improvise strange and abstract moves, rhythmic or atmospheric sounds, which help the actors to experience aspects of the world of the play, such as danger, misery, jealousy or sensuality. This is largely a matter of finding the clues in the text and then working in the space to embody the atmosphere suggested by each scene. An example could be the ensemble creating jerky disconnected movements and a cacophony of percussive and vocal sounds to underscore the banquet scene in *Macbeth* (Act 3 Scene 4) where Banquo's ghost throws Macbeth into confusion, so that the actor playing Macbeth is not asked to manufacture an extreme emotional reaction to the appearance of the ghost, but is able to

respond directly to stimuli which actually do confuse and disorientate his senses.

2   To give strong physical and vocal responses, in the moment, to whatever the principal actors say and do: In this way these actors can experience an amplification of their own power to change and affect the world around them. This is very important for actors feeling their way through a text, and can help them gain ownership of the text and a clear sense of its meaning and force.

To use the ensemble creatively to provide activities, agendas, atmospheres and contexts for actors, exploring text should be standard in rehearsal even when there are only a few cast members. In the training process it is essential. In the early stages of training you will not yet have learned how to sustain energy and breath in a state of physical stillness, nor how to respond to the minutest changes in each other, nor how to feed off each other's emotional energy. However, you will be able to respond to clear and vigorous physical tasks and strong visual and vocal stimuli which get the breath into the body and keep you mentally focused. By ensuring there is enough to do and see within the space it is possible to prevent you from disappearing into your own heads and closing down your bodies. Keep present, keep in the moment, keep doing, is the best advice for actors who are trying to own their text.

You may worry that working the text through the ensemble takes you away from what you perceive as the main task of the actor, which is to discover how to play the text in front of an audience, often using fairly conventional staging. The fact is, however, that your journey towards performance will not be, and should not be, a straight line. Some actors never progress very far beyond their initial interpretation of the character at the readthrough, which makes for a very tired and bored rendition. It is a good thing even for an experienced actor to take a roundabout journey towards finding the character, to try many things which may not ultimately be used in performance, but which will help in the process of 'layering' the character. It is a relatively easy task to shape something which is alive and growing; it is harder to breathe life into something mechanical and dead. Working through the ensemble is both a useful training technique and a rehearsal process which you will be able to use throughout your career.

9

Inhabiting the Space

Within the training or rehearsal environment there are many other ways of using the space and the ensemble in the space, to create simple physical contexts in which the text can be effectively and truthfully played with. These contexts can be matched to the given circumstances of the play, or to the characters themselves. They are not fixed techniques but examples of how the offers and the text can be played out in a highly absorbing physical situation which serves to bypass self-consciousness, inhibition and the simple refusal of the body to connect impulsively to unfamiliar words and situations.

You may at some point have experienced self-conscious-ness in the space due to an awareness of being observed. It is the same feeling that the child in the classroom gets when he has been playing the fool and suddenly realises the teacher is behind him. Stanislavski talks about the awkwardness which the whole theatrical situation creates in the actor, and the paradox that it is only when you feel you are no longer being watched that you can relax and become natural in your actions.

Like it or not, one of the key features of drama is that it is observed, whether by the audience or by the camera. Some amateur actors confront this problem with a very up-front, showmanlike style – the 'I'll get them before they get me' approach. Others studiously ignore the audience, concen-trating entirely on their scene partner, but because they lack training they tend to shut out the audience both physically and vocally, making the performance a private rather than a public act.

One of the best ways to avoid either extreme is for you to develop a continual professional consciousness, not of the audience, but of the space. No matter how intimate the scene, there is always an aspect of it which is offered outwards to the space. I always remind my trainees that every time they speak they are making the air vibrate in the furthest corner of the studio which is how it should be. If you think in terms of offering to the space rather than directly to the other actor's face, then a lot of habitual problems can be avoided. One tendency for actors is to invade each other's personal space, especially when getting heated in a scene. They end up practically nose-to-nose, with nowhere to go, and with the audience almost entirely excluded from the scene. This is odd, because one rarely sees such behaviour in real life, even in drunken stand-offs.

To some extent the space can be seen as the third person in a two-person scene. The space has an identity; the space confers or withholds permissions. Even in real life the dimensions, ownership and location of spaces dictates much of our behaviour. You will not behave the same way in a church as you do in a nightclub. You might think nothing of having sex in your own apartment, but feel strange about doing it in your grandparents' house.

The nature of spaces is not fixed, however, and this is what makes the space almost like another person. You can fight for ownership of spaces, or for permission to do things in them, and if you win then the nature of the space may change for you. The throne room may begin as a symbol of your oppression and end as an icon of your power, or vice versa, as in *King Lear*.

The problem with the theatre space is that someone else usually owns it, and, whoever owns it, the stage management claims control over it. It may make you feel like a barely-tolerated visitor in the space, or you may be terrified of it. One of the first duties of the actor trainer is to help you see the space as a dynamic, magical and unpredictable entity, not a sacred temple in which you are too scared to touch anything. You also need to dismantle any sense of fixed hierarchy of spaces. The nature of the theatre space should be conferred upon it by the actors and the world of the play, not by the fact that one space happens to be in the National Theatre and another in a room above a pub. The training studio is as much a space, your peers as much an audience, as in any formally designated theatre.

OWNING THE SPACE

Put simply, the actor needs to *own* the space, while the character needs to *negotiate* with it. If you own the space then you will see the audience rather than yourself, as the guests. A good hotelier will charge guests to enter his space and while they are there ensure they are offered everything they need, while still retaining ownership of the space. He should not behave like a private householder and either ignore, or resent, or be scared of the guests! As an actor you are the same. You offer out to the space everything that the audience needs, but you still own it.

It is because of this ownership that you can allow the space to take on new identities, some of which may involve symbolic qualities or personalities. *A Doll's House,* as the title indicates, is set in a fictional space which by its very nature represents ideas of control and disempowerment. Torvald may see the room as an extension of the doll-like identity he imposes on Nora, a sort of fantasy world he can retire to at the end of a long day. She, on the other hand, may view it (at least initially) more as a playground within whose boundaries she finds a kind of freedom. In either case, for you to have a sense of the room's symbolic identity will inevitably affect the way you respond to it, move within it and ultimately, abandon it. The identity of the room of course changes through the play, and the characters respond to these changes as fully as they do to each other.

By offering to the space and responding to the space, rather than just to each other, you can open up your performance and find the freedom and ownership of the space which relaxes you and extends your physical and vocal permissions. As a starting exercise when working on a scene I will often get the actors running round the room speaking their lines to the underside of chairs, to windows, to the inside of pianos, or whatever they can find, using the textures of what they touch, the physical positions they get into and even the smell of objects, to influence how they speak the words.

These exercises not only give you physical confidence and stop you seeing the space as a formal or ritualised area, they also start to break the habit of fixed eye-contact which so many trainees seem hooked on. It is not that eye contact, or more general visual contact with a scene partner, is a bad thing – it is just that its use should be dictated by the action and not by your habitual practices.

As in the *Macbeth* example in the last chapter, getting you working physically in the space should ideally involve working with the ensemble. This is not only invaluable to the actors working a scene, but also excellent training for those in the ensemble in working outside of a specific character and within the group context. Just as the space can symbolise aspects of the characters or their relationship, so the ensemble can reflect, amplify and enhance such aspects, turning them into dynamic physical realities. In the exercise outlined below, as in *Macbeth*, the ensemble plays out Nora's secret rebellions, while Torvald has to deal with a space in which everyone seems to be working to deceive him behind his back.

The Moving Statue Game

The group remains still for the most part, spread around the space, some standing, some sitting, crouching, lying down, all in tableaux. Every so often a random individual moves, travels a short distance across the space and then freezes again. The job of the actor playing Torvald is to try and catch and block these moves, while Nora's job is to encourage them (without words) to move while Torvald's back is turned. Neither actor can touch the ensemble. Once the actors feel familiar with the physical game, they start to vocalise, using short learned sections of text from the opening scene of the play, which they deliver within the context of the game.

The role of the ensemble here is to represent in magnified form aspects of the characters' worlds. For Torvald the ensemble symbolises Nora's excesses, and he can both respond physically to them and speak the text to them. For Nora the ensemble represents all the little subversions and tricks which she uses to get her own way within his constricting regime, but which she can also disown when she needs to. At times the actors find themselves speaking the text from within a particular physical activity; at other times the demand of the text makes them change physical direction or the manner of an activity. In this way the text and the physical happenings in the space begin to have an interactive relationship.

At one point, for instance, Torvald tries to get Nora to admit she has been eating sweets – a forbidden activity:

> TORVALD (*wagging a finger at her*). Surely your sweet tooth didn't get the better of you in town today?
>
> NORA. No ... how could you think that?
>
> TORVALD. Didn't Little Sweet-Tooth just look in at the confectioner's?
>
> NORA. No, honestly, Torvald.
>
> TORVALD. Not to taste one little sweet?
>
> NORA. No, of course not.

All through this speech, the actor playing Torvald continues to look out for and actively suppress the subversion in the 'moving statues', so that his lines are spoken within a strong physical context of authoritarian behaviour, On the other hand, the implied tone of the text forces him to use a benevolent and paternal approach to the physical task. Hence the physical work gives the actor a sense of how far Nora's disobedience taxes Torvald's sense of order, while the text forces him, within that context, to be paternalistic rather than angry. If the actor playing Torvald allows the ensemble within this game to represent further aspects of the play, such as Krogstad's insolence and his own insecurities, then he can experience directly the stress of Torvald's life, and the sheer effort he puts into maintaining control of others.

Nora, on the other hand, finds a need to be doubly careful, during this section of dialogue, not to be caught encouraging the ensemble to move and annoy Torvald. Since she is trying to protest her innocence, she has to ensure that whenever

Torvald looks directly at her, she is nowhere near any ensemble members, while at the same time moving quickly to encourage them whenever his back is turned. Her text flows from the physical urgency, and we can see that this dialogue, far from being a gentle and teasing ritual within a successful marriage, exposes a fault-line in the relationship which is revealed more fully later in the act.

An exercise of this kind also allows you to explore in a physical sense the notions of 'control' and 'subversion' within the opening scene of the play. It does not create the scene, but it gives you a greater understanding of the dynamic of the scene and the 'child/parent' relationship set up within the marriage. In a very physical way the actor playing Torvald comes to understand what it feels like to be in a world where everyone else is constantly up to mischief, behaving like children and constantly in need of discipline and correction. In an equally physical way the actor playing Nora manages to subvert his authority and takes a very childish delight in so doing. By experiencing the physical dynamic of their relationship both actors are later able to encapsulate a certain energy and physicality in the space even when working on their performances in a much more 'naturalistic' way.

A word here about the ensemble. The training methodologies in this book emphasise that within the space you should always be switched on to what is happening around you, open and responsive. This includes the ensemble. As an actor within the ensemble you should not only be responding to other ensemble members, but also feeding off the principals and reacting to what happens, even if this is within complete stillness and silence. That way the principals will in turn be able to feed off the atmosphere and tensions created by the ensemble, who are, after all, part of the totality of the space. Whether the ensemble is being used merely as a rehearsal technique or whether it is carried into the performance, your job in the ensemble is both to create atmosphere and to reflect what you receive from the principals back into the space in an amplified form. An ensemble which is weary, or unresponsive, or merely going through the motions, can destroy the atmosphere of a scene as effectively as one which is energised, responsive and focused can create it. Everything that happens in the space is significant. By understanding the material significance of the fictional space and responding to its atmosphere, you can free up your physicality and learn to move on impulse.

10

Learning to Trust the Body

I mentioned earlier that nothing happens outside of a context, and it is only by fully understanding, committing to and working organically within a clearly understood context, or world, that actors find freedom. Give an actor an infinite number of choices and he will be confused and disorientated. Restrict the number of choices to just a few and he will spring confidently into life.

Like morality, then, freedom is not an absolute concept. In fact it is largely an illusion constructed in the individual mind. If you feel yourself to be free then you are free, and one of the freedoms which the human mind and body could be said to offer us is the ability to perform background tasks without thinking about it. If our conscious minds had to remember how to do everything from breathing and digesting food to the exact sequence of muscle movements required to iron a shirt, we would soon collapse from the enormity of the task. Managing and running a human being twenty-four hours a day is simply too complex a job for any conscious mind to take on. Fortunately, we don't have to do it that way. Most bodily functions are performed without our even realising they are happening; while during our lifetimes our bodies learn to perform a multiplicity of tasks which we never again have to think about. We can drive a car, brush our teeth, make dinner, with our thoughts entirely elsewhere.

Why is it then so few actors trust themselves to perform tasks without thinking about them? Many seem to feel that unless they are consciously thinking about their lines, their moves, or their next emotion in Scene 3, they will simply not be able to function. The truth of the matter is that acting, like real life, relies on you trusting your body and unconscious mind to do most of what has to be done, so that the conscious mind can be focused on the moment.

The next exercise can be used in rehearsal for a scripted play once you have learned your lines. It allows you to trust your body in a context which also minimises the cost of failing. It is based on the idea that within most dramatic productions you have to understand and accept the parameters within which you are working. One example of a parameter is the text itself, from which in most cases you may not stray. Further examples of such parameters are: the director's vision of the piece, blocking, the designer's set and the costumes. Your own research, understanding of style, period and convention may add still more. As a professional actor you do not worry about parameters, you merely accept them. Out of role you may want to discuss costume, moves etc, but in the space your acceptance must be total, otherwise your resistance will communicate itself to the audience and make your performance hesitant and untruthful.

Within this exercise you have three distinct tasks. The first is to take a piece of written text and a clear set of physical instructions, and practise these until they can be performed easily from memory. The second is to allow yourself to perform the instructions in the space without thinking about them. The final task is to work with and respond to another actor, so both the set moves and text are performed within a dynamic context.

The Tableaux Exercise

A pair of scene partners takes a short section of learned text from their scene – say one page of dialogue. Between them they select five moments in this section, consisting of the opening moment, the closing moment and three points in between. Using an exaggerated and heightened style they create tableaux for each of these moments, based on the kind of physical/status/spatial relationship which they feel the text suggests. For the moment we are still working in an abstract space. Once the tableaux have been decided upon, each pair of actors practises the sequence and the

movement from one tableau to the next until the
sequence of tableaux becomes almost second nature.

What happens now is something of a leap of faith. The actors
are instructed to start with their opening tableau, and
instead of moving directly to the second, to improvise
physically (without words and possibly to music) within the
broad context of the scene and the characters, keeping aware
of each other and responding to each other on impulse. The
movement impro can be based on notions of status and
spatial relationships. The actors can also be encouraged to
explore different levels and to lead with specific body parts,
to break them out of habitual movement patterns. At all
times they must be aware of each other's presence, even
when visual contact is momentarily broken. There is no time
limit. The only proviso is they must at some point in the
sequence pass through each tableau, in order, and finish with
a freeze on the last one. The idea is to achieve this without
contriving or forcing it, but by letting it happen.

The passage laid out below is an example of how this exercise might work, if two actors were using part of the scene
from Act 3 of *A Doll's House* in which Mrs Linde proposes
marriage to her former fiancé, Krogstad. It should be stressed
that the tableaux described in this example are possibilities
only:

Tableau 1 *Mrs Linde stands tall. Krogstad is half on the
floor trying to pull away from her, but she holds him back.*

MRS LINDE. I've learned to think before I act. Life and bitter
necessity have taught me that.

KROGSTAD. Life has taught me not to believe in fine speeches.

MRS LINDE. Then life has taught you something valuable. But
you must believe in deeds?

KROGSTAD. What do you mean by that?

Tableau 2 *Krogstad is on all fours. Mrs Linde sits astride
him, trying to make him look at her.*

MRS LINDE. You said you were like a shipwrecked man
clinging to a spar.

[110]

KROGSTAD. I had good reason to say so.

MRS LINDE. I'm like a shipwrecked woman clinging to a spar – no-one to cry over and no-one to care for.

KROGSTAD. It was your own choice.

Tableau 3 *Both Krogstad and Mrs Linde are on the floor, she clinging to his leg, he trying to pull away again.*

MRS LINDE. There was no other choice at the time.

KROGSTAD. Well?

MRS LINDE. Nils . . . suppose we two shipwrecked people could join forces/

KROGSTAD. What do you mean?

MRS LINDE. Two on a spar would be better than each of us alone.

KROGSTAD. Kristina!

Tableau 4 *Mrs Linde and Krogstad are facing each other, standing knees slightly bent, holding each other with both hands and outstretched arms, supporting each other's weight.*

MRS LINDE. Why do you suppose I came to town? –

KROGSTAD. Were you really thinking of me?

MRS LINDE. I must work or life isn't bearable. All my life, as long as I can remember, I've worked – that's been my one great joy. But now that I'm alone in the world I feel completely lost and empty. There's no joy in working for oneself, Nils . . . let me have something – and someone – to work for.

Tableau 5 *As though Krogstad has let go of Mrs Linde, she is in a huddle on the floor, he standing back from her.*

krogstad. I don't trust that.

Between the tableaux the actors can improvise their movement freely, but are encouraged to do so in an abstract rather than naturalistic way. What this means in practice is that they find a heightened expression, in their bodies and in their spatial relationship, for those aspects of the dialogue concerned with status, emotional offers, emotional connection and attitudes to one another. The lines of the dialogue are conditioned by the physical relationship.

Most actors when first given this instruction are doubtful whether they can do it without consciously manipulating the movement, but they need to be persuaded the tableaux can happen quite organically provided they relax into the improvisation and allow themselves to work without anxiety.

Surprising though it may sound, most actors manage to find the tableaux quite naturally without trying. The main reason for failure here is usually that they don't trust themselves, and are working with excess tension. For those who find the tableaux relatively easily there is a good actor's lesson to be learned. Most of what an actor does in the space is dictated by the subconscious, in the same way that in life you do things on 'automatic pilot'. You do not need to think about much of what you do, because these are *learned tasks*. You do them without thinking, leaving your conscious minds free to focus on that which is new and different – the book or newspaper you are reading, the conversation you are having, the plans you are making for the holidays, or whatever. If you are worrying about what the next line is or how you are going to reach the right emotional state for the end of the scene, you will be too tense and inward-looking and therefore unable to exist in the moment. You have to trust that the things which have been *fixed* have also been learned and will happen of their own volition. You need to focus on that which is *not* fixed – the things which will only be decided in the moment. Unless you trust yourself to do what has to be done at the right moment, you will try to control everything with your conscious mind, and the result will be a disconnected and halting performance, the result of overloading one part of the brain and ignoring another.

Once you have found the tableaux for the first time, the confidence to find them again, even with an entirely different physical journey, will increase. It is at this point that you can begin to add the text of the scene. The actors are given two pieces of advice:

> Remember this is not a performance. Don't try to make it into one.

Speak the text from where you are, not with fixed intonations.

You are allowed to take as long as you like to deliver the scene provided that as you reach the different tableaux you also reach the moments in the text from which the tableaux were originally taken.

With growing confidence in your ability to find moves and lines without thinking, you can afford to focus on other actors and on the space, expanding each impulse into a heightened or even abstract physical gesture. In so doing you may discover, quite by chance, physical moments which affect the way the text is spoken. For instance, two actors working on the final act of *A Doll's House* might reach a point where Torvald is hiding under a chair from a rampaging Nora just as he speaks the line 'You frighten me, Nora', which he is able to do with perfect truth in that moment. The point here is not that the actors are discovering abiding truths about the play or how to perform it, but that they are discovering that only by trusting themselves to speak from the physical and emotional context of each moment, can they have total ownership of the text. Of course they are neither the first nor the last to speak this text, but because the *context* in which they speak is unique to them, to their scene partner and to the moment, in that moment the text belongs to them.

The tableaux exercise, like those in previous chapters, gives the actors the permission to build a physical dynamic which is drawn from the text but driven by them, and to let the text ride on that dynamic. Once again, the actor, not the text, drives the action.

At some point, of course, if the actors working on this play wish to take it forward towards actual performance, they will have to come to terms with another set of parameters – those of the physical space in which each scene is located. These of course include the furniture, doors, windows, props etc which will usually be present in a production, but more importantly the formalities and social rituals which the physical space represents. By the time you reach this point, you will already have explored the text within a number of different contexts and parameters, and this should theoretically be just another context. Provided you have the self-confidence to see these new parameters as a new and interesting playground within which to work, you should respond to this new world with enormous energy. By now you will be used to a much greater level of physical and spatial freedom than that offered by nineteenth-century middle-class conventions, so, although you have to accept the conventions without question, you will also be constantly working at the edge of your permissions, occasionally overstepping and pulling yourself back or being pulled back by others. As a result the performances will most likely be energised and full of humanity and a deeply visceral sense of desire and need. What the audience will see are caged animals trying to break out, not trained circus animals going through the motions of social rituals.

To reinforce this quality, I often let actors, when they first get onto the stage set, start off without any social constraints whatsoever. Given the permission to treat the space as a group of monkeys might treat a playground, still more discoveries are made, and the text finds homes in all sorts of new places and contexts. Again, these are not about faithfully delivering Ibsen's play; they are about you working outside of the social permissions which the world of the play gives you, so that when you are brought back within those parameters you will feel the strain. This process of blocking off options can happen bit by bit rather than suddenly, so that you find yourself constantly hitting new boundaries and having to change direction. In this way, the audience can gain a strange and intangible sense that Nora would actually like to roll on the floor when she tells Mrs Linde how happy she is; that Krogstad would like to put his foot through the Christmas parcels; that Dr Rank would like to seize Nora and make love to her, or whatever. The reason the audience can identify these impulses is because you have actually given yourself permission to do these things in rehearsal. The exact nature of the impulses is not important; what matters is the sense of bottled up and rechannelled energy at work within each actor.

As a result of exercises like this, the energy in performance is actually your physical memory. Each time you walk into the space and see your scene partner, you become aware of what you have been through together – you remember in your body all the experiences which relate to these characters and this scene, and it is that intensity which creates the physical subtext.

What is crucial about this is that you *need* the memory of your rehearsal exercises because you haven't actually lived through the characters' personal history and experience of each other. The rehearsal exercises can in some measure compensate and substitute for the real experience of Nora and Torvald's eight-year marriage, which of course you can never actually live out. For this reason it is very important that in rehearsal you really explore their relationships and create the inner life of the play by using your own humanity and complexities. We do not go to see *A Doll's House* in order to sneer at the naivety or rigidity of nineteenth-century society; we go so we can witness the way in which both men and women try to negotiate power within existing power structures and to observe the point at which those structures have to be challenged. Only when you have really explored the parameters of your world in a physical as well as imaginative way; only when you have not just understood but experienced what it means to be restricted in unfamiliar ways, can you really inhabit this world without thinking, without trying. This is the point at which your thought-processes and efforts start to work entirely within the world of the play.

11

Voice and Movement

There are all too many misconceptions within the industry about what voice training is, why we do it, and what an actor should sound like. A few generations ago there were still many voice teachers who aimed for the 'declamatory' voice, encouraging actors to drop their pitch by an octave or so and to speak all lines in a kind of over-articulated and heightened RP. There is no doubt that actors so trained were able to express very clearly and to the back rows of large theatres a whole range of 'theatrical' emotional states, and their performances were often very powerful. Powerful, that is, in the sense that an audience could all too easily respond emotionally and empathetically to the kind of air vibrations produced by such voices. It is arguable, however, that the modern actor requires a different and altogether more versatile set of vocal skills to equip them for work in today's industry.

In Aristotelian terms, the main purpose of serious drama is the purging of the emotions of pity and fear through catharsis, a massive empathetic surge taking the audience up to a climactic moment, which for the character is a tragic death, and for actor and audience is a kind of emotional orgasm. In this sense the ritual of drama could be seen as a kind of social therapy which prevents the building up of neuroses and tension within a community. It fulfils roughly the same function as certain religious rituals; indeed, Ancient Greek theatre, like the medieval theatre in Northern Europe, grew out of religious ceremonies.

Drama in our society can also be about empathy and recognition, but in terms of social ritual it bears little resemblance to either Ancient Greek or Renaissance drama. The nearest thing one could find to that sort of mass theatre in our society is probably the football match, which has the same 'purging' effect, providing spectators with a channel for quite a huge outpouring of physical and vocal emotion, including song, chanting, exultation and lamentation.

Much of our drama no longer fulfils this function within society, possibly because most of it is no longer experienced within the context of a mass audience. The majority of modern dramas, whether written for stage or for television, are not structured like classical tragedies, and are more likely to be holding the mirror up to particular aspects of daily life than constructing an epic story about the tragic downfall of an individual. In the late twentieth and early twenty-first centuries we are probably more interested in 'everyman' – the person in the street – than in kings and emperors.

For this reason you need to train your voice, not just for delivering great tragic speeches – although those skills may still be valid for some performances – but also for expressing a whole range of much smaller emotions. While an audience's attention can be grabbed using vocal resonance alone, it can only be *held* by constant changes (for example in pace, pitch, intonation and volume) which the audience can clearly understand as precise thought changes happening within the dramatic context. We all have the capacity to respond minutely to what is in front of us, but the capacity to translate our smallest responses into clear and readable vocal choices in a performance situation is a skill which for most has to be learned.

Practical voice training on an acting course therefore has to fulfil several functions. Firstly it has to teach you to breathe in an open and relaxed way, and to speak 'on support' without pushing or forcing the voice. To be on support means to have an easy intake of breath, combined with excellent muscular control in the chest, stomach and abdomen, which controls the release of air to produce an unconstricted and steady sound.

Secondly you must learn to extend your range of vocal choices or possibilities; thirdly you must be able to articulate each choice with pinpoint accuracy; and fourthly you need to connect voice and breath with thought, so that whatever idea or image is present in the mind finds its expression in the vocal choice, and conveys that image clearly and truthfully to the audience. For this reason voice training can never be a purely technical process. At every stage of the training actors need to work at least partly with text and language, whether dramatic text, poetry or other forms of prose, so that the actor has clear contexts in which to sound and articulate words, and clear images which need to be expressed.

In today's drama 'washes' of emotional quality or even carefully prepared vocal tapestries are simply not enough, because most of our drama requires you to negotiate the moment in a way which is not about theatrically heightened emotional states or grand demonstrations of inner conflict, but about the *journey* of the character through a dramatic situation. Just as in real life people live through situations by managing (for better or worse) each moment as it arises, so you the actor, although you already know the outcome of a scene, must still find a new route through the scene each time you perform it.

Of course, drama is not real life, and for the actor there is that extra factor in the equation, which is of course the audience. A fully-trained vocal instrument is the means through which the actor *communicates* each change in thought, feeling and strategy without forcing or demonstrating her reactions. If your voice does not possess that versatility, you may be able to live in the moment, but many of your responses will fail to communicate themselves. Not surprisingly, the vocal versatility of a well-trained actor also includes the skills required to work at different levels in different performance media. Once your vocal skills are properly honed, you will be able to communicate the fine detail of a scene in a fifteen-hundred seater theatre or in a television duologue. In the former instance you will have the unforced power to speak without shouting; in the latter you will be able to work at low volume without coming off support.

It is probably safe to assume that if human beings were still living in hunter-gatherer communities, in tune with their environments and bodies, they would have a very natural access to all the vocal qualities they needed, with no blocking, tension, or physical restriction. This is certainly the case with babies and young children. However, through thousands of years of social conditioning people have learned to block and conceal their natural responses to one another. Since the human ear is an acute instrument and highly sensitive to emotional qualities in others, the advent of overcrowded urban lifestyles has necessitated a further suppression of the natural voice, simply in order to maintain a little privacy among hordes of strangers.

For some people this can take the form of a constantly unsupported voice devoid of resonance or connection with the body. Emotion has therefore to be communicated through the 'extremities', via emphatic face, arm and shoulder gestures which in themselves create more tension and restrict the voice still further. When emotional states are expressed the voice will tend to become shrill and strangled, and the shoulders even more tense in a kind of vicious circle of head-jutting, squawking and tension whose meaning we might understand, but whose emotional quality leaves us cold.

Other people manage to maintain resonance and breath within a relaxed body, but conceal emotion through a dull and monotonous pitch and tone, or by repetitive tonal patterns which deliberately override the actual thoughts and emotions of the speaker.

In our everyday lives most of us probably feel safer with unsupported voices. They put us at less risk and they make fewer emotional demands on other people. A voice which lacks connected resonance implies muted emotions which are firmly under the speaker's control. We listen carefully for that vocal signal which changes the air vibrations and tells us there has been an important emotional gear-shift in the other person. If we hear no change, then we don't feel at risk. However, we might also get bored and stop listening.

Vocal habits can be so ingrained that we are not even aware our emotions are being suppressed or our responses to others are blocked. When we listen to other people, however, we are aware which voices force us to pay attention and which send us to sleep, just as the audience is aware of which actors grab their attention and which don't.

For the audience the theatre is not the place to feel safe. We come to the theatre to take emotional risks which we don't dare to take in real life. If the acting is good then we are transported into the world of the play, and within that world we experience an empathetic connection with the character. Within the totality of the theatrical experience the *voice* of the actor is paramount. No matter how much exploding scenery, wild lighting effects, emotive music and sizzling dialogue a performance contains, it is the emotional journey of the character which we follow, and it is principally through the voice that we follow it.

Much of the rest of this book deals with the practical processes through which you the actor can maintain dynamic and responsive relationships with other actors in the space. It also offers a series of contexts in which you can find the need to speak and therefore the incentive to access the full potential of your vocal instrument. However, it is important to emphasise that none of these are of much use unless you have already inwardly consented to freeing your voice and using it flexibly and truthfully. Strong vocal technique is one of the key factors which enables actors to stay in touch with one another in the space and to feed off each other's energy, so the need to force emotion or invent responses is removed. If you begin your training with a trapped voice, you will need to address the problem before you can really begin to understand the training processes and make progress as an actor.

The training of the voice itself takes place outside of acting classes, and is a practical process which can only be achieved through good teaching and constant practice. Most actors also find it useful to underpin their vocal training with a sound knowledge of vocal theory and anatomy. There are many excellent books available on the subject, including those of Kristin Linklater,[12] Barbara Houseman,[13] Patsy Rodenburg[14] and the later works of Cicely Berry.[15]

Practical voice teaching works best in a group context, preferably as part of a drama-school training. There are many excellent voice tutors available, but there are also many whose teaching methods are outdated and geared to producing a particular vocal quality rather than to freeing the natural voice of the actor. There is no way of assessing the quality of a teacher other than by trying them out, but for those studying in the UK it is probably safe to say that voice tutors who have the Postgraduate Voice Studies qualification from Central School of Speech and Drama will at least be starting from a sound theoretical base.[16]

MOVEMENT

Hand in hand with voice training, and inseparable from it, is the training of the body to move in the space. Traditionally actors have been trained very separately in voice and movement, but in fact it is very important for these skills to be seen to be overlapping and interdependent. The actor needs to have a strong sense of the relationship between voice and the body, because the connected voice is both affected by the movement of the body and is a key factor in movement impulses. Without this two-way relationship the actor will either become very static – what we call 'neck-up acting' – or will move in a way which is clearly not connected to voice, breath and thought, which makes the performance seem awkward and inorganic.

Getting the breath into the body is the first step in finding the voice/body connection. This is most easily achieved simply by getting the body moving, and many of the acting exercises in this book are designed to create vigorous physical contexts within which the actors can speak. However, the next step concerns the openness and versatility of the body in responding to stimuli both from the actor's own voice and from the other actors' offers in the space. Most actors have inbuilt tensions and physical defences at the start of their training which to a greater or lesser extent impede the body's organic responses and lock the actor up physically. The first duty of movement training is to free up the body, because if you find yourself unable to respond organically in the space then you could easily panic and start to force the body into disconnected and demonstrated moves as a survival strategy.

The more you do this, the harder it will be for you to break the habit later in the training. For this reason movement training needs to focus above all on physical *release.*

What you must first understand is that your habitual physicality is not about who you naturally are as a person; it is largely about the choices you have made throughout your life in response to situations you have encountered. There may be certain features of your physicality which stem from your basic physiology, but the capacity for physical development during a training programme, through fitness, muscularity and reprogramming of the body's physical memory, is vast. The process of achieving this, however, can be uncomfortable, and some actors resist it, particularly where their physical habits are rooted in fears and neuroses. It is important therefore, that the movement programme is carefully constructed to allow you to achieve release gradually and without being pushed too far out of your comfort zone too soon.

By the time children reach adolescence they have usually become acutely and self-consciously aware of the fact that their bodies are constantly transmitting signals to others, and that some of these signals are sexual. Unlike younger children, teenagers are terrified of the vulnerability and exposure which accompanies bodily signals, but unlike adults they are not yet in control of their own body language. As a result many adolescents attempt to 'shut down' their body signs and their spoken language so they expose as little as possible, especially to adults. Some sit hunched up in 'hoodies', speaking in a monotone and restricting themselves to stock phrases. Most avoid gestures which betray emotions of any kind. Since mind and body are constantly affecting and being affected by each other, this closed physical and verbal language leads to closed thinking, until the adolescent is convinced that this way of being represents the totality of her identity, rather than being a series of social choices which she has the power to change.

While most actors starting a course of professional training will have moved beyond the extremes of adolescent behaviour, many will be left with restricted vocal and physical vocabularies, and will have little idea of their own potential in these areas. The circular relationship between expression and self-awareness will tend to perpetuate these limitations, which means that initial movement training needs to work on two levels – the *cognitive* and the *visceral.* In other words, you need to choose to take on new physicalities ranging from the concrete to the abstract and inhabit these through physical memory, but you also need to be aware of the cultural context of the language you are using, and of how your signals may be read, so that your physical vocabulary will develop within clear social parameters. Ultimately you should learn to move on impulse without censorship while at the same time being physically precise and specific and having access to a wide range of moves and gestures.

Practical movement work for the actor starts simply. At the outset your aim is to discover both the sensation and the language of the still and neutral body. In some ways the concept of the neutral body is an oxymoron, since the body will always signify something even when it is at its least expressive. In the world of actor training, however, the concept of neutrality tends to refer to a posture, whether seated, standing, lying down or whatever, in which the body is held as far as possible in symmetry and spinal alignment, and muscular tension is at the minimum level required for sustaining this posture. In other words, neutrality is a position rarely assumed in an everyday social context, since it is relatively hard for observers to detect specific social signs or reactions in the neutral body.

To exist in neutral on a daily basis in early movement classes is essential for lifting you out of habitual gestural patterns, especially awkwardness and fidgeting, and allowing you to experience your body as something more akin to a blank canvas. This has the dual effect of giving you permission to make new and different gestures, and of making those gestures precise and clear, emerging as they do, not from a random clutter of awkward social mannerisms, but from stillness and neutral presence. In neutral states you need to be aware, not just your external appearance, but how the rhythms of your body, such as heartbeat and breathing, originate in the body's centres and emerge as energy on the body's surface. In this way you can begin to understand how all movement initiates from an impulse, and how the external form which that movement takes is merely the outward expression of something which began deep within the body.

For you to reach this awareness requires continual and steady 'reprogramming' of the body's habitual pathways, and this process can only be achieved through exercises which compel you to make new physical choices and to build your awareness of these new pathways so that your physical vocabulary is constantly growing. The body can easily learn, with practice, new ways of moving and responding, just as we learn to ride a bike or play the piano. The difference in this case is that you will not be learning just a few specific new moves, but working to achieve a broad physical vocabulary which will allow you to work organically and without censorship using many different forms of social convention and character archetype.

Movement impulses almost always arise from an interactive context rather than from the body in isolation. This can be either the interaction of the body with the space, or, in common with many of the acting exercises in this book, interaction of the body with other bodies, either in pairs or as a group. These situations provide contexts in which you can physically negotiate status, contact, spatial relationships and gestures ranging from the abstract to the specific. In this way you will learn to follow physical impulses fearlessly, teaching yourself to avoid well-trodden pathways and seek new ones. Little by little you can dismantle the restraints and censorship which your life experiences have put in place and find out how to use your body openly and responsively. To achieve this you have to put aside any preconceived notions of grand purpose and massive emotional outpouring. Responding to others on an abstract physical level is a simple consensual process, not a heroic drama. In movement as with acting and voice you must simply work within your parameters and make choices in response to what is offered.

Actors studying movement will find that not only does the movement studio offer them the processes through which they can understand their bodies, but also a specific permission which is conferred upon them by the space. You will find yourself able to move in abstraction, to heighten and hone your physicality and to release into the body, in ways which you could not have allowed yourself outside that space. This is a wonderful and liberating experience, but of course you will ultimately have to take those permissions out of the movement space and into the voice space, the acting space, the singing space and of course the performance space. For this reason it is essential on any course of actor training that skill areas overlap, and that each tutor demands of the trainees aspects of the skills being developed in other disciplines. For example, it should be clear from the descriptions of acting exercises in the rest of this book how important it is for you to work outside the realms of everyday behaviours and physicalities, and to play around with impulse and abstraction in spaces which give wider physical permission than the 'naturalistic' set. By using the permissions and the language of the movement space, you can open yourself to a whole new range of rehearsal possibilities and develop dynamic strategies to help you physically engage with the text.

Voice and movement sessions could be described as the 'engine room' of any actor training. It is through these sessions you will discover the expressive and communicative potential of your body in all its aspects, which you can then bring into the more specific and defined contexts of the playtext and the performance. You ignore or sideline your basic vocal and physical training at your peril, since however great your potential as an actor, at some point you will find, to your frustration and dismay, that without sound technique you simply do not have the resources to do what you want to do.

12

After Meisner

Sanford Meisner (1905-1997) was one of the group of American actor-training practitioners, including Lee Strasberg and Stella Adler, who from the 1920s studied and adapted the teachings of Stanislavski. Like Strasberg and Adler he later founded his own school (at the Neighbourhood Playhouse in New York), where apart from a brief period as a Hollywood actor he spent most of his working life, retiring only in 1990.

Meisner differed from Lee Strasberg in that he did not believe that the Stanislavskian principle of 'affective memory', which formed the basis for Strasberg's Method, should be central to an actor's art. In other words, although Meisner expected his actors to be emotionally open, he placed more emphasis on the truth of the moment and the actors' organic impulses and responses to one another than on weeks of character research and emotional preparation. Indeed, although Meisner never specifically rejected the idea of the 'character' as something which could exist outside of the moment, he placed the emphasis squarely on the 'reality of doing' as the main signifier of character. In other words, it is the audience, not the actor, who makes the final judgement about who the character is.

The central plank of Meisner's training methodology was the 'Repetition Exercise'. In its various forms this exercise could be used to free up an actor's impulses, powers of observation and honesty of response. Repetition begins as a simple improvisation exercise and gradually becomes more complex, up to the point where it can be used as part of the actor's work on a character.

Just as Meisner would not have regarded Stanislavski's System as sacred, so this book does not attempt faithfully to reproduce Meisner's theories, but borrows some of his basic principles and builds on them. Some of the early exercises described in this and the ensuing chapters come directly from Meisner; others derive from his ideas but have been adapted or developed to work within a wider training programme. The most valuable aspect of Meisner's work in this context has to be the insistence on the actor directing his focus away from himself and onto other people.

Affecting others and being affected by them on a moment-by-moment basis is what we do naturally in real life, and if actors are to convince us that what we are seeing mirrors the human processes of real life then that is also what actors must do. Unfortunately, doing what comes naturally may be easy when no-one is watching us, but when we get in an acting space it suddenly becomes extremely difficult. Meisner's exercises are designed to present actors with simple observation tasks which help them forget themselves and concentrate on the situation they are involved in.

Simple Repetition

The most basic repetition exercise, this is something which the actor can do at any time, in or out of the teaching space, with one other person. We start with two actors observing each other, not just using direct eye-contact, but taking in each other from head to foot. After a while one of the actors (it doesn't matter which) makes a spoken observation about the other, which in the first instance must be entirely factual. The other actor repeats the statement back, but makes it about herself, as we see below:

ACTOR 1. You've got red socks on.

ACTOR 2. I've got red socks on.

ACTOR 1. You've got red socks on.

ACTOR 2. I've got red socks on.

And so it goes on, with the comment never changing.

When you first try this exercise you may try to impose all sorts of things on the line – trying out different voices, tones etc. for dramatic effect. I often have to stop the exercise and explain to actors that they should not impose, but just keep saying the line within the situation, letting whatever physical and vocal changes which occur happen in a natural and unforced way. It may take you a while to stop 'acting' and accept that the exercise is really as simple as it seems. For this reason you will have to do the exercise for quite a long time before you relax into it. You may also reach a point of boredom where you stop trying and just mechanically repeat the line, or a point of laughter where you just see the absurdity of the whole thing, but provided you keep watching each other, these can be seen as a natural part of the process. Eventually you will get to the point where you are so desperate to find something to respond to that you will enter a new level of observation and focus, and things *will* start to happen, but these will be within the context of this relationship and not imposed from without. We are not talking great dramatic changes here, but very small and intimate responses, which the group watching will be able to read and recognise as truthful reactions.

Simple repetition is also an excellent way of achieving focus at the beginning of a session and changing the atmosphere within the space from the rather random and wide-angle awareness of the whole group to a very specific and concentrated mental focus. It is amazing how quickly, when given a simple task of this kind, you can narrow your observational lens and, without needing to shut anything out, give your whole attention to the situation before you. Since the line of text you are using is so simple and unchanging you can afford to let yourself completely alone and allow all changes to be governed by your observation of your partner rather than contriving change within yourself. It is the beginning of a *habit* of looking outwards rather than inwards, of finding all instructions in the space rather than in yourself.

Three-Moment Repetition

Once the actors have become used to simple repetition, and can work without inventing anything, they can try out three-moment repetition. This starts in a similar way to simple repetition, but then something different happens, as follows:

ACTOR 1. You've got a rip in your shirt.

ACTOR 2. I've got a rip in my shirt.

ACTOR 1. You looked at it.

What has happened here is that the first actor has made a comment and the second actor repeated it, as in simple repetition, but at the point where the second actor heard the comment she had an involuntary physical response, which the first actor noted and immediately commented on. At this moment the sequence ends, and the third comment is not repeated. At this point either actor can start the whole process again, and so it goes on.

At first you will need to restrict your comments to the purely factual. This is because before you have really got used to being honest about what you see there may be a tendency to manipulate or invent rather than comment. After a time, however, you may be allowed to extend your observations, as in the example below:

ACTOR 1. You've got a spot on your nose.

ACTOR 2. I've got a spot on my nose!

ACTOR 1. You didn't know that.

What Actor 1 has done is to observe Actor 2's reaction, and comment on the most obvious element of what he saw. This isn't quite a factual comment, but it is truthful to the extent that he is working entirely from observation and not from conjecture or his own imagination. The only problem about allowing such comments is that sometimes you may be tempted to manipulate the situation, as in:

ACTOR 1. You're looking at me.

ACTOR 2. I'm looking at you.

ACTOR 1. You fancy me.

At this point I would stop these actors and point out the flaws in this exchange. To begin with, the initial observation 'you're looking at me' is problematic, since the fact that Actor 2 was looking at Actor 1 was a given within the situation. However, Actor 2 repeats it as expected. At this point, Actor 1 starts to work not from observation but from a desire to manipulate the situation, possibly to embarrass his partner, and the exchange ceases to be truthful. It is essential within three-moment repetition to maintain that honesty and not to give in to the temptation to play power-games with your partner. Otherwise the dialogue loses touch with the reality of the moment and each actor starts to live in a different world from his partner. The experience for the audience will be one of disconnection and concealment of real impulses.

Three-moment repetition tends to maintain a greater intensity than simple repetition, because you will always be looking to seize upon the reaction you observe and articulate it as immediately as possible. In order to avoid superficiality both in the reactions and observations, however, it is necessary to breathe properly. Otherwise this can turn into just a party-game and will rarely shift out of 'fun' mode, nor will it really challenge you.

Occasionally, the mere fact of having reactions observed can make you 'freeze' in your attempt not to give away any involuntary responses. To avoid this I often insist that at the end of each block of three statements, both actors have to break eye contact, move and then re-establish contact after a few moments. This helps you avoid the 'rabbit in headlights' freezing up which can result from the experience of having your every move observed. Eventually you will realise there is nothing all that terrifying about allowing your uncensored responses to be noted in the space. On the contrary, it is these very involuntary responses which are the stuff of truthful and engaging acting.

Standard Repetition

Standard repetition starts in the same way as simple and three-moment repetition, but then keeps changing as the actors observe things changing in each other:

ACTOR 1. You're shuffling your feet.

ACTOR 2. I'm shuffling my feet.

ACTOR 1. You're shuffling your feet.

ACTOR 2. I'm shuffling my feet.

ACTOR 1. You're shuffling your feet.

ACTOR 2. You're smiling.

ACTOR 1. I'm smiling.

ACTOR 2. You're smiling.

ACTOR 1. You're rubbing your nose.

ACTOR 2. I'm rubbing my nose.

And so on. The comments don't have to change as quickly as this, and in fact it's probably best if they don't, because if the actors feel they must keep changing the comment then they will spend too much time trying to find something new rather than just allowing themselves to observe.

As with the previous exercise, you should at first stick with the strictly factual rather than trying to comment on what the other person is thinking or feeling. As you get used to the idea of seeing and commenting without manipulation, gradually you will be able to allow yourself to respond to the emotional changes which occur in your partner. We are not talking great bursts of emotion here, but simply the way you perceive that your partner has responded. For example:

ACTOR 1. You raised your eyebrow.

ACTOR 2. I raised my eyebrow.

ACTOR 1. You raised your eyebrow.

ACTOR 2. You're amused by that.

ACTOR 1. I'm amused by that . . .

Again, initially both you and your tutor should beware of observations which are manipulative rather than truthful. Manipulations occur where one of you decides to *try out* a comment to see how the other will react, rather than honestly observing it. Sometimes these are not easy to spot. One actor I saw working said 'you're ugly' to her partner, which might have been construed as a manipulation and outside the rules of the space, but turned out to be a genuine spontaneous observation. The best way to spot manipulations is through the voice and breath. If you are breathing openly, and not catching the breath or using over-long pauses, the observations are more likely to be honest. If you shallow breathe and are clearly holding defensive tension in the body or face, it is more likely that manipulation is happening. Sometimes this is a deliberate attempt to stay in control; at other times it is happening because the free flow of observation and comment have been obstructed.

The other common form of manipulation happens when you are actually not interested in observing at all, but are using the exercise to 'tell a story', making comments which deliberately force the other person into a certain role, and direct the relationship between them. This way of working is useless, because it shuts down the possibility of genuine interaction and keeps all power and control securely in the hands of one person. Your partner soon realises she has no chance of affecting you because you are not really watching her, and she therefore shuts down, making the whole exchange lifeless and meaningless.

You should be able, after a few sessions, to abandon both your defence mechanisms and your desire to create exciting dramas, and simply respond. Once you are secure with your technique, it is possible to embark on 'extended' standard repetition. This entails a continuous session of up to an hour, working with the same partner without coming out of the exercise even for a second. This gives you the opportunity to discover a whole relationship and an intimacy, within the rules and structures of the repetition format. Whenever I run this extended version of the exercise with a group of actors, two things become very apparent. Firstly that it is possible to have six pairs of actors working in quite a small space without anyone feeling intruded upon, because the focus within the pairs is so strong; secondly that the actors involved cease to be aware of the passing of time. Often when I have stopped the exercise after an hour and told the actors how long they have been working I am greeted with disbelief.

The hour-long session (and it could easily go on longer), besides being a way to get you relaxing into the technique, is a useful reminder that in drama it is not fantastic stories which create and hold interest, but the actors' involvement in what they are doing. The simplest of narratives can be absolutely fascinating provided the actors themselves appear fascinated by it. The most fantastical of tall tales can be empty and lifeless if you don't engage with it. You can discover this not just by doing repetition exercises but also by watching them. It is in that key moment where you have observed something in your partner and been affected by it, and where we the audience are waiting for a couple of beats for the response, that dramatic tension lies. Most audiences like to feel that the action of a dramatic encounter is unfolding in the here and now, not that it has been rehearsed and emotionally 'mapped' beforehand. Even with limited text, Meisner exercises can be engaging to watch, and it is that immediacy and your genuine vulnerability in the space that lies at the heart of the theatrical experience.

In terms of your craft, the only problem which this kind of repetition presents is that although it leads to a level of truth, focus and intensity between two people which can be highly effective on camera, it does not necessarily work in a theatre context, especially when viewed from a distance. What becomes necessary at this stage is to get the responses into the body and into the space, so the connection is not just perceptual and psychological, maintained through stillness and eye contact, but can be read through the whole body. However, it is important this does not happen too soon. The whole point of repetition is to take the actor's focus off himself and to some extent off the audience, and onto his scene partner. If the actor is reminded too soon in the process of his responsibilities towards the audience then the repetition will become superficial and demonstrated, with the real focus being elsewhere.

Physical Repetition

We can start to achieve a more physical approach to repetition without making the actor self-conscious, by closing off certain options within the space and by introducing a physical dynamic from the outset. In other words, the repetition starts with a particular physical relationship and develops from there using standard repetition. Examples of these relationships include:

- Actor 1 pins Actor 2 to the floor or the wall

- Actors 1 and 2 lean towards each other, their weight resting on each other's palms

- Actors 1 and 2 lean backwards onto each other

- Actor 1 climbs on Actor 2's back

- Both actors lie on their sides, facing one another

... or any other physical situation which implies through spatial relationships and body positioning a certain sort of emotional starting-point. What is important in this type of repetition is that the actors should not immediately try to extricate themselves from the physical situation and thereby re-establish 'normality', but instead work with the situation so when it changes it does so as a result of the relationship changing, and instead of the actors backing off from each other they continue to engage physically, so that the physicality continues to reflect the relationship.

As with other forms of repetition, it is crucially important that you continue merely to observe and comment rather than manipulate, although the comments may be about what the other person is doing to you, as in: 'you're supporting me' or 'you're pinning me down'. If you start to say things like 'you're a bully' or 'you need to let me go', then the exercise ceases to be about your observation of the other person, and begins to be about your own emotional reaction to events. In repetition I try to avoid letting actors use defensive emotions to wriggle out of situations, because these have a tendency to shut you down and stop you engaging with the relationship. Everyday life is full of situations where we become defensive with each other and refuse to allow anyone else to affect or change us, but most dramatic scenes are about those key moments in which change *does* occur. Your job is to allow that change to happen organically, in the body, rather than simply demonstrating or 'faking' it in the head.

WORKING WITH AGENDAS

The next stage in repetition is to add basic agendas to the standard repetition exercise, so the actors are not just randomly observing, but are doing so with an underlying purpose which they take into the space. To reach this stage actors must have left crude manipulation tactics behind; otherwise they will have a tendency to use these in order to pursue an agenda.

At this point I have heard actors ask 'well why can't we manipulate? – people do in real life!', and up to a point they are right. The difference is that in real life there are *consequences* to manipulating someone, which might make you think twice before doing it. In the repetition exercises there are no consequences other than you stop truly observing and start 'shaping' the other person, which removes the risk to yourself, and puts you firmly in control of the whole proceeding. If both actors are manipulating then the whole exchange loses any connection and truth, and all an audience will see are two immovable people getting nowhere.

As I mentioned in Chapter 7, the 'agenda' is something which replaces the Stanislavskian concept of 'objective' or 'task', in much the same way that in Transactional Improvisation the 'offer' replaces the 'action'. So how is an agenda different from an objective? The difference lies in the directness of it. Some Stanislavskian actors talk about 'playing an objective' – others even call it 'working an objective' – but either way there is a rather one-track directness about an objective which doesn't really allow for side-tracking. And yet side-tracking is at the heart of most human intercourse, and certainly is a fundamental principle of TI, with its offers and counter-offers. To return for a moment to the scene from *Macbeth* we looked at in Chapter 7: if Lady Macbeth's objective is to get Macbeth's compliance with the murder scheme, and if she plays this objective like a ping-pong player bashing balls back at her scene-partner, then the scene becomes rather one-dimensional, because what the actors are not taking into account is the fact that *all* objectives, in real life as in drama, are *negotiable* within the scenes where they are played. In other words, the scene is not just about whether a particular fixed outcome is agreed or not agreed, but about whether that outcome stays the same throughout the scene, whether it still matters by the end, or indeed whether it ever did. Very often, as in the Lady Macbeth scene, the apparent objective may well be masking something much more complex and indefinable within the marital relationship. One might even decide (though this is just an idea) that Lady Macbeth has moments where she would *like* her husband to rise up and assert his authority, and that were he to do so her objective would cease to matter. How much more interesting if we can let the audience see that the bloody power-struggle which develops within this play derives at least partly from the sexual and psychological power-struggle within the marriage. How much more fascinating if the huge political events which follow can within this exchange be observed hanging by a thread, subject to the physical chemistry of two people.

In short, the concept of the objective is too linear and simplistic to serve dramas which from Euripides onwards seek to show us more complex layers of human transactions. By contrast, the *agenda* is a much more malleable and alterable quantity, which does not sit in the front seat of the action but is an underlying driving force, one which is not 'played' or 'worked' but '*allowed*'.

At the start of a scene, the agenda and the objective may appear to be very similar. The agenda is what the character intends to achieve at the point where the scene opens, and the strength of the agenda, as with the objective, will define the energy level which the character brings into the space. After that, however, events take over, and the agenda retires to the background, from where it can continue to *drive* and *energise* the action, but not *shape* it. At some point in the scene the actor may realise that the agenda has changed, and so it can, but not necessarily all at once. There is a clear example of this in the H.E. Bates novel, *The Darling Buds of May*, where Charlie the tax inspector finds his initial agenda of sorting out Pop Larkin's tax arrears is gradually transformed into something entirely different as he is seduced both by the Larkins' lifestyle, and by Pop's daughter Mariette. In this story, the initial agenda and the events in the space do battle with each other, but an actor would find it hard to decide exactly where the agenda finally loses the battle, nor should he need to. The agenda is simply something he returns to whenever the events in the space loosen their grip slightly.

This in a nutshell is what the agenda is – *the outside circumstance which defines our opening moves, and which continues to drive us until such a time as our experiences in the space give us reason to abandon it.* Thus it may be with Krogstad in *A Doll's House*, who enters at the start of Act 3 presumably with the intention of giving Mrs Linde the full benefit of his bitterness and desire for revenge. Once he realises that she is offering to marry him, the agenda wavers but does not entirely disappear. Again, it does battle with events until finally it gives way, but the exact progression of that battle is up to the actor in the moment.

In other scenes, the agenda remains in place, because nothing that happens in the space actually challenges it. Even if this happens, however, the agenda can take 'detours' which temporarily reshape it and give the audience a sense that it could change. In Act 1 Scene 2 of *Richard III*, Richard may have the agenda to persuade Anne to marry him, and he may continue to pursue this agenda until the end of the scene and beyond, but there may also be moments during the scene when other things might happen between the two of them, arising from the nature of the language and the intimacy of the exchange, which could lead the actors and the audience to forget the stated agenda and see something different happening. I have seen a version of this scene in which Richard became so emotionally involved in this intimacy and so vulnerable to Anne, that it took quite an effort of will to bring himself back to his original agenda once she had gone. For a few moments he allowed the audience to see his humanity, and to believe that perhaps the story could take a different direction.

To return to the Meisner exercise: the first repetition exercise involving agendas works as follows:

Repetition with Activity and Agenda

This is a form of standard repetition in which one of the actors has a simple ongoing physical activity which to begin with is their main concern. This could be anything from

stacking and unstacking chairs, to removing and rethreading
her shoelaces – the point being that the activity must be
one which the actor can perform easily but it must also
require at least a modicum of attention and physical
choice. Actor 2 has no activity but has an agenda, which
must be centred in Actor 1. An example might be that
Actor 2 wants Actor 1 to see and comment on her new
trousers, or that Actor 2 wants Actor 1 to give her a hug.

Once you have an agenda, it becomes very hard to resist
manipulation. Comments such as 'you're not looking at my
trousers' or 'you're not hugging me' start to come out, which
as negative statements have no real validity in repetition. You
might as well say 'you're not an elephant'. Similarly, 'you're
looking at my trousers' is also inadmissible unless you genuinely believe it to be so. What you have to understand here is
that the agenda is not the same as an objective. You do not
come into the space with a single objective which drives you
through the scene. You arrive with an agenda which gets you
through the door, and what you do from that point depends
largely on the other person. When Isabella arrives in Angelo's
office to plead for her brother in *Measure for Measure* she is
initially quite half-hearted about the whole proceeding, and
quite prepared to accept Angelo's curt refusal. One might say
that her agenda is not to save her brother's life but to prove
that she can't. Once she arrives in the space, however, it is
possible that she perceives something in Angelo that makes
her stay and argue the case. It is impossible to say what that
might be without being there in the moment, but what can
be said is that even the strongest agendas cannot be
translated into objectives because the action in the space
invariably takes over from the outside circumstance and
redefines in each moment what the actors want from each
other. If the action in the space does not become more
absorbing and watchable than the original objective then we
the audience are likely to stop watching. There is nothing
more dull than an actor relentlessly pursuing an objective by
speaking the text with a single-minded persistence regardless
of what the other actor is doing.

So we persuade Actor 2 that the agenda can be there without it forcing us to break the rules of the repetition game, which say we must observe and comment rather than manipulate. If you follow this rule, the exchange might go something like this:

ACTOR 2. You're stacking chairs.

ACTOR 1. I'm stacking chairs.

ACTOR 2. You're stacking chairs.

ACTOR 1. I'm stacking chairs.

ACTOR 2. You're stacking chairs.

ACTOR 1. You're in my way.

ACTOR 2. I'm in your way.

ACTOR 1. You're in my way.

ACTOR 2. I'm in your way.

ACTOR 1. You want something.

ACTOR 2. I want something.

ACTOR 1. You want something.

ACTOR 2. You've stopped stacking.

As Actor 2, by keeping the focus off yourself, it is possible to let your agenda influence your physicality and tone of voice, while staying open within the exchange and experiencing it from within rather than standing back and manipulating. For you the key thing is the relationship itself, without which the agenda is meaningless and empty. Here, as it should be, the scene gives meaning to the agenda rather than the objective giving meaning to the scene. Having the agenda at the start of the scene offers you a series of new pathways and possibilities within the scene – it does not force you down one road.

As Actor 1, on the other hand, you are pursuing the activity, but the activity, like the agenda, is something which you continue to do in the background, can pause from and return to when the exchange momentarily loses interest for you. It keeps you in the space, stops you feeling self-conscious and both reflects and influences the tempo of your responses. What you should not do is hide behind the activity in the manner of 'I can't listen to you now, I've got to finish this'. You need to be open to Actor 2, and in this you are assisted by the need to keep repeating.

The completion of the activity and the fulfilment of the agenda are of course irrelevant, or at least their importance is not absolute but relative to whatever develops between the two actors in the space. What is of real importance is, as ever, the actors' growing ability to let the three strands of the *agenda*, the *activity* and the *repetition* blend together in a unity of circumstance, with the actors' attention shifting from one to the other in an unforced way, prompted from within the space rather than within the actors' heads.

This exercise has the effect of changing the repetition from something intensely personal, involving a lot of two-way eye-contact, to something which exists within a specific space and context. The actors now have a greater permission to move within the space and to break the eye contact, which in turn forces them to be aware of each other in different ways.

Repetition with Obstruction

One of the most powerful versions of 'agenda' repetition is where Actor 1 has an agenda which is also partly an activity – to obstruct Actor 2 physically throughout the scene, whatever Actor 2 tries to do. In this case Actor 2 will normally have a simple activity such as measuring the room with his feet, which he keeps trying to achieve.

What happens, of course, is that the activity is constantly disrupted by the agenda in a very physical way. We note that it is not Actor 1's agenda to hurt or attack Actor 2, only to obstruct. The repetition continues throughout, and what we start to notice is that the observations become very much about the physical relationship. Comments such as 'you're holding my leg' start to come in, so that the observations are not just what Actor 2 perceives in Actor 1, but are also expressions of how Actor 2 feels in that context. Actor 2 must be careful not to become defensive or curl up in a metaphorical ball. Everything apart from his actual activity must be about identifying what Actor 1 wants from him and finding a way through.

Obstruction repetition is extremely useful for opening the plane of repetition games into a realm of physical conflict which reminds the actors of what it is often so easy for them to forget – their own physical vulnerability and the ways in which they can use their bodies and voices to try to gain a psychological advantage in a physical situation. It also removes the option of working from the head and shutting out what is happening, since either the frustration of being obstructed or the implacable cruelty of doing the obstructing are physical facts which cannot easily be avoided – in fact it is the actor's job not to try and shut out what is happening, but to let it affect him.

As the name suggests, repetition must be done over and over again for it to begin to change your habits in a way which will translate into a performance situation. Repetition games are however the most effective and painless way to bring about these essential changes that I have ever encountered. They bypass barriers and create a space in which you can work openly without fear. However it is very important that you allow yourself to *do* the exercises rather than questioning them. Caution, reserve and suspicion are major stumbling blocks in any training exercise, and for this reason I never attempt improvised repetition exercises until actors have already been in training for a year, by which time most of them have gained not just emotional openness but also released bodies and voices through which the repetition exercises can really resonate.

13

Approaches to Text – Part Two

Meisner's repetition exercises tend to be used mainly as ways of training the actor to respond more honestly and spontaneously in an improvisation situation, the idea being that the habit of 'reading and responding' will translate itself into text-based situations. However, it is also possible to use repetition on text, in a number of different ways. Later in this chapter I will outline some of the methods through which repetition can be used in the early stages of rehearsal to find a way into the text. The early part of this chapter, however, deals with the actor's initial preparatory work on a text, and the methods used to find a personal connection with a character and a situation.

Actors have a tendency to see the text as something outside themselves, created and therefore owned by the author rather than the actor. For this reason they see themselves as a conduit for the author's creation, and the text itself as a fixed entity. This perception is of course strengthened by the existence within the canon of 'definitive' performances by great actors, which imply there is only one really sound way to play a text. I have often heard experienced acting teachers criticise a actor's performance, not because it was incoherent or inept, but because they didn't agree with the interpretation of the text. In other words, what they were looking for from the actor was a restatement of their own preconceptions (or possibly a carbon copy of the way they themselves played the role twenty years before!).

My view, however, is that the text starts to belong to the actor from the moment you pick it up. That is not to say you do not have a responsibility to study and explore the text and its background, and to avoid imposing anything onto it which may work against it, but any group of actors performing a text must have made it their own or their performance will be very dull to watch.

When you read the text and explore its social or historical background, you immediately begin to create images and ideas in your head about the nature of the story and characters, and about the encounters the characters have. At this point, however, you may not *feel* ownership – the text is still an alien thing made up from somebody else's words – and the journey has only just begun. The character which you intend to play, and the journey that character goes on are still just free-floating concepts, and you are still experiencing all moments of the play simultaneously. What you now need is a *process* through which you can get inside each moment and experience it to the full.

THE FIVE-POINT TECHNIQUE

This process begins with the 'five-point' text-preparation technique, which again is a technique derived from Meisner but not identical to it. This technique has the following aims:

1   To locate the scene for the actor firmly in time and space, and to understand the character's place in the narrative in terms of status, relationships, history and defining characteristics.

2   To separate fact from conjecture, making the actor clear about what is actually established and what is just assumed on a first reading.

3   To make some clear opening decisions for use as starting-points in rehearsal, so that the actor's initial offers are clear, strong and consistent with the text.

You first identify the 'scenes' which your character appears in. A scene is defined as the point where the character comes on up until the point where the character goes off. Beyond that there are no further divisions. A scene can be one line: 'the carriage is at the door, sir' or it can be twenty pages.

The five points which you then have to identify are as follows:

What my character does during the scene

The trick is not to be too specific, or too unspecific. The level of detail might be as follows: 'My character enters with a bunch of flowers, gives them to the maid to put in a vase, talks to the gentleman in the chair about the weather and about how unlucky he is, before going out, stumbling against a table as he goes.' This account takes in the key activities in the scene without quoting the entire text. Writing this down enables you to strip away your preconceptions about what actually takes place in the scene, which might well be coloured in your mind by later events which at this point haven't happened yet.

What my character knows at the start of the scene

Also known as 'The Knowledge', this is a totally factual list of things the character knows for certain at the *start* of the scene. It does not include anything the character finds out during the course of the scene, although you may have to search the whole text to find out everything your character knows at this point. For instance, if the play were a murder mystery, and your character was the murderer, he would know he had committed the murder before anyone else did, although this information might not be revealed until the end of the play. The list should also include very obvious things, such as 'My character knows he is entering the dining room', since little facts such as these can sometimes be overlooked. The point behind this list is that sometimes actors confuse what the character knows with what *they* know, or mistake conjecture for fact. With the list in place you have a clear picture of what your character actually knows for sure, and from this can work out what the character does *not* know, which can be equally important. In a play like Chekhov's *Three Sisters*, for example, it is all too easy to assume that all the characters have heard all the conversations, when in fact some characters may be oblivious to certain information because they weren't in the room at the time.

The Knowledge also requires you to define the relationships between your character and the other characters, in a purely factual sense. In a Shakespearean history play, The Knowledge will include such facts as 'Queen Margaret is my character's aunt'. In another play it might be essential to know that someone is your character's boss, or is engaged to your character's sister. Depending on the play, The Knowledge can be a very long or a very short list, but provided everything in it can be shown to be solid fact, it will all be useful.

What my character's agenda is at the start of the scene

This is something I dealt with earlier. The agenda is of course the reason for the character being in the space. It isn't always as obvious as it may seem. For instance, the actor playing Lopakhin in Chekhov's *The Cherry Orchard* may assume that the character is there at the start of the play because of his desire to see Ranyevskaya again after five years, but a closer look reveals that he is there in order to persuade the family to adopt his business scheme for the orchard, a very different agenda which gives him a very different energy. As stated in the last chapter, the agenda can give way to other things, including, in the scenes that follow, pleasure and emotion at the reunion with Ranyevskaya. There are other distractions too, such as the budding relationship with Varya, but as we know, the agenda remains in place for most of the first two acts, after which it becomes redundant, and is replaced by another agenda.

What my character's need is at the start of the scene

Quite a difficult concept, which you may take some time to grasp. The 'need' is something which lies at the opposite end of the spectrum from the agenda, in that the agenda is a clear and rational concept while the need is a metaphysical notion which suggests a lack, or imbalance, in the character, of which the agenda is merely a symptom. The need is expressed not as a simple or literal objective, but as a metaphor or image. To return to the example of Lopakhin: if his agenda is to convince Ranyevskaya of the merit of his scheme for holiday homes, thereby saving the orchard and their inheritance, then his need might be expressed as 'he needs to bury the child'. This is less confusing than it sounds. Lopakhin is a wealthy businessman, but he has very strong memories of his peasant childhood, of beatings, a debt owed to Ranyevskaya, and of his sense of lowliness. These are all described in the text. The interesting thing about the need is that it can have multiple meanings, and, because it is unspecific in terms of whom it relates to, it can alter its context according to the scene. In the first and second acts Lopakhin may be trying to repay Ranyevskaya for her earlier kindness to the abused boy, thereby settling the score and allowing him to 'bury the child' by moving on. In the third act Lopakhin, having given up on Ranyevskaya, 'buries the child' by buying the orchard where he was once a peasant boy, but also, by driving Ranyevskaya out of the orchard, sets her free from the place where her own child was drowned, something he knows is haunting her. To have a child 'unburied' at the start of the play gives Lopakhin a restlessness and a mission which goes beyond a mere agenda. As with the agenda, however, this need does not have to be at the front of the actor's mind, although there are some exercises I shall describe in a later chapter, which show how the need can be used in the space. The need is just 'allowed' to be there.

However metaphorically the need may be expressed, it has absolutely no meaning outside the situation of the play, and it entirely relates to the transactional status game which underlies all human intercourse. Lopakhin's need is not connected to some great moral battle, nor does it define him as a character – it is something created by his changing social status, and more specifically by his immediate surroundings during the play.

What is my 'as if' for this need?

The 'as if' is *not* the same as Stanislavski's 'magic if' and the two should never be confused. The 'as if' is a means by which you can find a personal connection with the *need* which you have identified for the character. It is called the 'as if' because it is *not* a search back into your past to find a parallel situation to the one in the play; instead you find the 'as if' by asking yourself what situation could conceivably arise in your life at some point in the *future* which might awaken the need you have identified. To return to the Lopakhin example – if the identified need is 'to bury the child', you might imagine (for example) that in your own life you meet someone whom you haven't seen since childhood, who makes assumptions about you, and treats you as if the intervening thirty or so years have never happened, completely negating all your achievements and developments. You do not have to imagine or conjure up any emotions with regard to this 'as if' – you merely have to recognise the imaginary situation. If this particular situation rings no bells then you must find another. Once you have found a parallel situation – in the future not the past – then you can let it form part of the 'layering' of your conscious and unconscious awareness of the character's situation. You do *not* need to sit in the wings each night conjuring up this situation and the accompanying emotions before going on stage. The 'as if' is merely a way of giving you a personal insight into the ways in which this character might perceive his world, by relating the character's need to your own emotional drives. Finding the 'as if' is the first step towards transferring ownership of the character from the author to the actor.

The five-point exercise, parts of which might take considerable thought and searching for the right means of expression, will help you gain a fuller and more specific understanding of the character in its most basic form as words on a page, without trying to fix the character or impose ideas on it before you have even stepped into the rehearsal space. The next stage, however, is to use *text repetition* to help you own not just the broad notion of the character, but the specific words which the character utters. Text repetition is also very useful for getting other actors to listen, which in turn allows you to feel that the words are alive and useful within the space.

Text Repetition

This is a technique for using the words of the text as repetition in a way that turns the words into the currency of the moment in almost the same way as the improvised observations of standard repetition.

Text repetition might go something like this:

Act 1 of *The Cherry Orchard*

DUNYASHA. We waited and waited . . .

ANYA. You waited and waited . . .

DUNYASHA. We waited and waited . . .

ANYA. You waited and waited . . .

DUNYASHA. We waited and waited . . .

ANYA. I didn't sleep on the way . . .

DUNYASHA. You didn't sleep on the way . . .

ANYA. I didn't sleep on the way . . .

DUNYASHA. You didn't sleep on the way . . .

ANYA. I haven't slept for four nights . . .

DUNYASHA. You haven't slept for four nights . . .

The text is broken up into phrases, which shouldn't be too long, otherwise you will find it hard to repeat them. Actor 1 speaks the first phrase, Actor 2 repeats it, and it goes back and forth in the same way as improvised repetition. In this case, however, only the actor who has the *next* line or phrase in the text can change the phrase. As with standard repetition you have to find a reason to change the phrase, and that reason must be found in the person you are talking to. Similarly, while a phrase is being thrown back and forth, it has to find a meaning in the context of the relationship as it is in each moment, otherwise the whole exchange becomes meaningless.

The need to repeat the other actor's lines and the need to repeat your own lines over and over again means that if you are to avoid just mechanically intoning the words, you have to listen and observe, just in order to find out how to speak the phrase each time. At the start of the scene it is clear that Dunyasha has been very impatient to tell Anya the news that Yepikhodov has proposed to her, but when Anya says how tired and cold she is, Dunyasha has to deal with that information before she can move forward. She cannot move the subject on to her own preoccupation until she has found a reason (or a permission) to do so, in Anya herself. In other words, she has to deal with Anya's tiredness. She might find physical ways of doing this, such as taking off Anya's outer clothes or helping her take her hair down, but she is waiting until the moment is right to talk about her proposal, which means that through the repetition she is observing Anya to see how receptive she is. It may be, of course, that Anya just becomes more and more weary and tearful, in which case Dunyasha could decide to give her the news in order to cheer her up, but whatever the permission Dunyasha gives herself, it is through the terms of that permission and its accompanying offer that the line will be spoken. Text repetition offers you the time to explore each moment at a stage where you are still feeling your way into the text and relationships, and do not quite know how to interpret what you observe in terms of the play and characters.

Text repetition stops you from getting stuck in a rut in which you speak your lines in the same way every time you rehearse a scene, and in which you stop listening to your scene partner. It can also help you become familiar with the words themselves, and force you to start using the text to affect others. Actors who use this technique in the early stages of rehearsal report that it enables them to find a connection with their scene partners and to gain ownership of the text much more effectively than trying to 'play the scene'. Furthermore the repetition is clearly a preparatory exercise rather than an attempt at performance, and it removes you far enough from the performance situation to allow you to work in a more relaxed and involved way, without trying to 'perform', but instead working to affect your scene partners. The experience of affecting someone else in the space is an intensely powerful and absorbing one. Because your partner is repeating everything you say, and because the way they repeat changes each time in direct response to you, a relationship develops almost at once which starts to build a context in which the words can be spoken. Once the actors have a sense of that context and the issues within it then the words cease to be a problem and become a tool.

Interpolated Repetition

This is a form of repetition which brings the text together with improvised repetition. The actors work from the text, without using text repetition as outlined above, speaking the words as they are on the page within the given circumstances of the play. However, every time the actor who is speaking sees his scene partner do anything significant, he breaks off from the text and comments on it in exactly the same way he would in standard repetition. However, he does this in character and in the context of the moment.

In this example from David Mamet's *Sexual Perversity in Chicago*, Bernie, an over-confident predatory male, is approaching Joan in a singles bar.

BERNIE (*pause*). So here I am. I'm just in town for a one-day layover and I happen to find myself in this bar. So, so far so good. What am I going to do? I could lounge alone and lonely and stare into my drink or I could take the bull by the horns and make an effort to enjoy myself . . .

JOAN. Are you making this up?

BERNIE. So hold on. So I see you seated at this table and I say to myself, 'Doug McKenzie', there is a young woman', I say to myself, 'What is she doing here?' and I think she is here for the same reasons as I. To enjoy herself, and perhaps, to meet provocative people . . .

Using interpolated repetition, the section might run as follows. The original text is in normal type; the interpolated comments are in italics:

BERNIE. So here I am. I'm just in town for a one-day layover and I happen to find myself in this bar . . . *you're not looking at me*

JOAN. *I'm not looking at you.*

BERNIE. . . . So, so far so good. What am I going to do? I could lounge alone and lonely and stare into my drink . . . *you folded your arms.*

JOAN. *I folded my arms.*

BERNIE. . . . or I could take the bull by the horns and make an effort to enjoy myself . . .

JOAN. Are you making this up?

BERNIE. So hold on. So I see you seated at this table and I say to myself . . . *you licked your lips!!*

JOAN. *I licked my lips!*

BERNIE. I say to myself, 'Doug McKenzie', there is a young woman', I say to myself, 'What is she doing here?' . . . *you're clutching the table!*

JOAN. *I'm clutching the table.*

BERNIE. . . . and I think she is here for the same reasons as I. To enjoy herself, and perhaps, to meet provocative people.

Mixing Mamet's text with the actor's own spontaneous observations has the effect of *destabilising* the text, turning it from a well-formed finished product into an unpredictable and fluid set of possibilities which the actor mixes freely with physical and vocal signals and with improvised observations. The effect of this is to keep both actors on their toes, the one because he is constantly looking for signals from Joan, and the other because she has to listen to Bernie so she is able to repeat. Part of Joan's listening will be for vocal signals which indicate whether what she is hearing is just a set chat-up routine or whether Bernie is actually responding to her. Of course, the entire scene could be played (and I have seen it played so) as just a comic sketch of annoying male predator and uninterested female. However, it is far more interesting if the audience can sense that the actors are not just taking up set positions with regard to each other, but that they are both potentially vulnerable to whatever happens within the scene. Interpolated repetition, by making you vulnerable to your scene partners' actions and with your own actions exposed for comment, allows you to experience the tensions and uncertainties of standard repetition within the textual framework and given circumstances of a scripted scene.

What you should get from this is once again a sense of ownership. After a while the text and the comments merge into one, and you realise it is your own observations and comments which have been determining how the text is spoken, rather than any preconceived idea of the scene. Even if the repetition statements are then taken away, you will tend to continue observing and responding to one another, so the observations which you would have made are channelled into the body and into the text proper.

It is essential in interpolated repetition that you allow yourselves to be affected by each other in character and in context, otherwise you will have a tendency to deliver the script as the character and make the interpolated observations as the actor. The trick here is in the actor allowing himself to observe the other actor through the lens of the character and the fictional situation, and to comment from that place. This does not have to be forced, it just has to be allowed. Thus when the actor playing Bernie sees Joan lick her lips, he allows himself to interpret this action in a sexual way, because that, for him, is the context of the scene (at least in that moment).

Once you have relaxed with the technique, then the verbalisation of what you observe gives you a heightened sense of the other actor's responses. By forcing you to articulate what you see, the exercise transforms you from a passive observer into an active commentator. By expressing out loud how your partner is reacting to you, you thereby acknowledge your reading of that reaction and allow it to shape the way the next lines are spoken.

Repetition exercises of this kind should ideally be undertaken at an early stage of rehearsal, when you are familiar with the play, but have not really explored the character yet. In common with the exercises in the next chapter, the aim of these forms of repetition is to place the process of characterisation firmly in the context of the space and the other actors. Character cannot be created outside of the space because it has no meaning outside of the space. What the audience sees as character is a series of interactions and transactions which occur in the specificity of a particular moment and with a particular group of actors. In your own time you can work on voice and physicality, sift the text for clues and research the historical background of the play, but you cannot 'set' your character or performance, because these are dependent on the moment. You undertake repetition exercises in order to build a bridge between a new and unfamiliar text, and your own observations and responses. In this way the character can begin to emerge as a fusion between the author's words and settings and your own existence within the space.

14

Defamiliarisation

However interactive a relationship actors set up through these early exercises, in the stages of rehearsal which follow, it is all too easy for you to become fixed in your physical characterisation. What this usually means is that you have either (rather lazily) allowed your own habits and mannerisms to be translated, possibly in a slightly distilled and heightened form, into the character's; or that you have made some premature decisions about the character's voice and physical moves which are safe and which you therefore stick with. The problem with 'fixing' a character's physicality and vocality too early is that if you haven't tried out different options in rehearsal then you won't really have sparked off new and different responses in your fellow actors. You will therefore probably have sunk into a rut where the other actors know exactly what they're going to get, so stop responding, which means that little by little you will all disconnect from one another and start to do your own thing.

Fixed physical characterisations are the result of an actor's lack of faith in the way the 'chemistry' of the rehearsal space can combine with the actor's awareness of the 'given circumstances',[17] to build the character organically. Actors have a habit of over-intellectualising and trying to remain in total control over the development of a role. Unfortunately this is a very limiting technique, and will often mean that you miss creative insights in rehearsal. Ultimately it is not only the characterisation which suffers, but the 'world' of the play, which will lack atmosphere and consistency both in rehearsal and performance.

THE ARCHETYPE

This is a technique through which you can explore and
heighten physicalities and vocalities which lie well outside
your own habitual range without falling into the trap of
stereotyping and superficial mimicry. It also stops the work
on the role from becoming too internalised and psychologically driven. You start by identifying the social type into
which your character fits, and giving that type a name. For
instance, Lopakhin from *The Cherry Orchard* might simply
be 'The Businessman'. What you should *not* do at this point,
however, is to start playing a *stereotype*, a generalised bland
demonstration of how you think a businessman looks and
behaves. What you *should* do is extrapolate from the archetype and from any information in the text, a series of habitual gestures which seem to illustrate the mentality of that
social type.

There are many possible ways of finding these gestures.
You might use *observation* – watching people in public who
seem to belong to this particular archetype, and recording
their mannerisms. In this particular case, however, Lopakhin
is actually operating outside his own environment, and his
behaviour must reflect not so much his everyday transactional dealings, but the frustrations and social confusion of
trying to deal with a different set of rules and offers which
don't fit with his logic. What the actor needs to do here is to
work in rehearsal to identify and experiment with a series of
mannerisms which express these and other emotions which
the text suggests.

Examples of Lopakhin's gestures might include:

1   A habit of sighing loudly with frustration when
other people start talking about emotion.

2   A tendency to point to people and things he is
talking about.

3   A habit of using a lot of excitable arm gestures to
try to convince people who can't see his logic.

Once these gestures have been identified, however, you
should beware of trying to use them to create a character in

a vacuum. These are all *social* gestures which emerge from the character's particular relationship with his surroundings, not from any fundamental core of character identity, and as such, they can only be realised in context.

The way to employ archetypal gestures and make them organic is not to impose them on a scene but to allow them to emerge as the appropriate context arises. The text suggests many possible points where each gesture could come into play and others where they probably wouldn't. In rehearsal you need to be allowing the other actors to *stimulate* these gestural responses, so they only appear in a specific context. Moreover, the gestures are not set pieces – they may start just as *tendencies* and gradually get bigger as they become more organic. The key to this lies in your faith that once permission has been given for the character to respond in these unfamiliar ways, then the gestures will start to appear in context. Giving yourself that permission can be difficult, and it is sometimes useful for you to use costume or props to endorse the permission. What you must avoid, however, is imposing a physicality which doesn't take account of the specific information in the text or shuts out the responses of the other actors. A gesture which arises in response to situation and agenda can remain fluid and active, and will spark off other gestures; a gesture which is imposed on a character outside of a context will often be created through tension and will lock up the body's responses, both to the text and to everything the other actors are doing. This is the opposite of what the gestures are meant to achieve, which is to offer you a pathway of physical response to stimuli, so that what you observe in the moment finds an immediate and clear physical gestural expression. This in turn will both communicate to other actors and the audience, and give the actor making the gesture a strong sense of the character's social identity.

Since neither the chosen archetype nor the selected gestures in this case are fixed, the actor is at liberty to experiment by changing both the archetype and the gestures in order to widen the scope of his exploration. In the case of Lopakhin, he could try working with the archetype of 'the peasant', an epithet Lopakhin applies to himself. In this case the gestures might be:

1   A habit of adjusting his clothes as if uncomfortable in them.

2   A habit of looking at the floor when talking to people.

3   A habit of examining his hands as if not sure what to do with them.

Applied once again in *response* to others rather than as an opening offer, these gestures can open up for you yet another way of physically expressing your responses. It is important to remember, however, that you should not be in search of a 'holy grail' – a definitive way of playing the character. If you think you have found one, it is likely that your performances will be a lot less exciting to watch than your rehearsals. Techniques of this kind are simply a way of 'layering' the possibilities of the character, and creating a 'mini-past' for him, so that just as you in your own life have a social history which has conditioned much of your behaviour, so you the actor are conditioned by the rehearsal process into the behaviours which will ultimately define the character. The gestures themselves merely become part of the actor's 'response vocabulary'. Certain of these gestures will emerge at the forefront of the characterisation; others may fade away. Whatever is able to become organic will probably stay.

One actor I knew who took on the role of Fagin in a second-year production of *Oliver Twist* realised immediately that his own physicality was entirely inappropriate for a role whose circumstances differed in almost every respect from his own. The age, class, era and experiences of Fagin demanded that he explore a range of archetypes and the accompanying gestures, in order to avoid the pitfalls of playing a stereotyped 'miser'. Revisiting his previous *Commedia dell'Arte* work he took the archetype of *Pantalone* and used this as a starting point through which to find new gestures. From this he discovered several physical mannerisms – among them a habit of rubbing his hands together, and a tendency to put his face very close to people he wanted to talk to, as if to prevent others from hearing.

This actor also looked at the archetype of 'The Conjuror', who controls and manipulates with his hands, occasionally drawing attention to what one hand is doing, while the other hand subtly and secretly does something else. Having found these gestures the actor then realised he had to make them his own, and make them organic to the scenes and inter-actions of the play. As he explored further he found that the physicality he had discovered was not just a series of fixed mannerisms, but the outward manifestation of a whole social identity, through which Fagin conducted all his transactions. The gestures became flexible, adaptable and responsive. As the actor later reported:

> The exciting thing for an actor is being able to make so many different choices with the same movement. I found I could use the same gestures to mean different things for different occasions depending on who I was talking to . . . when Fagin's life had crumbled around him, I used the same gestures, but their shape and quality had changed. The free-flowing elegance had gone and instead had been replaced by a jagged sudden burst of movement, a wild swing . . . as if he was grasping at what was once him, but could not put it together . . . [18]

The gestures outlined above are physical, but you could equally be selecting vocal gestures and mannerisms which work for the character archetype. Vocal gestures include accent, articulation, pitch, pace, rhythm and resonance. Provided the vocal choices you make reflect the character's social background, status and transactional offers, strong vocal choices can often make the character archetype clearer. They can also affect your physicality, because certain vocal choices always have a social dimension, and therefore suggest accom-panying physical choices within certain social archetypes.

As with the physical gestures, it is important that you do not select and stick with a particular vocal choice, but experi-ment through rehearsal with a range of vocal possibilities, all of which bring different offers into the space and create dif-ferent dynamics with the other actors. As the offers change, so must the responses, so the actors are never allowed to settle into a particular way of playing but are kept constantly alert and responsive to one another. Of course, once the show gets near to performance you will need to settle for a certain range of choices, but within that range there will still be room for new things to happen, even halfway through a run.

THE UNDERLYING ACTIVITY

Another technique linked to the exploration of the archetype is the discovery of the underlying activity of the character. Based on an understanding of the character archetype, agenda and need, the underlying activity is a kind of physicalisation of the character's basic gestures into a simple and continuous activity which fits with the information provided in the text. If drama can be said to be 'interrupted ritual', then the underlying activity is the ritual which the action interrupts.

In the case of some characters identifying the underlying activity is easy. Christine the cook in *Miss Julie* only appears in her kitchen, and most of her ritual activities revolve around kitchen utensils. With Miss Julie herself it might be harder to identify the activity, but the one thing we know she does on the night of the play is dance. Although the text does not indicate that she literally dances in the kitchen, it might be a useful rehearsal exercise to use dancing as her underlying activity. Dancing can be flirtatious, frantic, feckless, rebellious, elusive, or any number of other qualities which might work for Miss Julie. To dance in the kitchen is also a social statement and an invasion of territory, forcing the manservant Jean to 'interrupt' her in a very physical way rather than just verbally; dancing is also highly energised, and would allow the actor playing Miss Julie to feel in her body the pace of the evening. It might not be the way ultimately to play the scene, but for the actress involved it could be a useful way of reminding herself in a very physical way of the emotional and sexual energy of the scene.

Having found the underlying activity, either for the whole play or a section of it, you now do two things. Firstly, you start to perform the activity within the space, using both the space and the things in it (if any) as part of the activity. Secondly, you play the scene from within the activity, making sure you find ways to observe and respond to your scene partners. At times the other characters might pull you out of the activity; at other times you might interrupt yourself and pause. It is up to you to decide what you can say and do from within the activity and what you have to stop for. At times you will be the 'interrupter' and at times the 'interrupted', either being forced out of your activity by someone else or taking the decision to pause your activity in order to deal with something or someone else. As an example, Miss Julie might stop her dancing in order to accept a drink from Jean, or Christine might stop her kitchen activities in order to pull Jean's hair affectionately. Similarly, characters might allow their interaction with each other not to *stop* the activity but to *change* the way it is performed. Christine might bang her pans on the stove or slam things down on the table in response to Jean's admiring comments about Miss Julie, or the tone of Miss Julie's dancing might alter according to Jean's responses to her.

The underlying activity gives the actor a clear physical and emotional context in which to play the scene. The moving body is far more able to register change and to be immediately and readably affected than the still body, in the same way that it is easier to turn the steering wheel on a moving car than on a stationary one. By reacting to each other from within a dynamic activity, actors can avoid the awkwardness or physical self-consciousness which comes from not quite knowing where they are. In other words, they have a context within which to respond.

THE ENSEMBLE VERSION

Where the play has a larger cast, the 'underlying activity' technique can usefully be expanded into an ensemble exercise, where the entire cast or training group all start to engage in their underlying activities around the space simultaneously, initially improvising outside of the context of a specific scene. When using this technique it is often useful for each cast member to take a handful of their character's phrases from the play which they can use freely and in no particular order to make verbal offers and responses in the space.

When I was working on *The Cherry Orchard* using this technique, the actor playing Lopakhin chose an underlying activity, within Act 2 (which is set outdoors), of 'surveying and measuring'. He had a pair of binoculars and a large tape measure, and throughout the act he measured up the space for holiday homes and access roads. Meanwhile Gayev was playing imaginary billiards; Ranyevskaya was looking for money (in her own bag and everyone else's pockets); Yepikhodov was playing the guitar; Charlotta cleaning her gun or taking aim at anything and anyone; Dunyasha trying to look like a lady; Varya looking for Anya; Anya and Trofimov hiding from her; and Yasha pretending to be a gentleman. In each case the actors chose three or four lines from their act which they felt summed up or worked well with their activity. Lopakhin's lines, for instance, were: 'The cherry orchard and the land along the river must be leased out for summer cottages'; 'I work all the hours God gave'; and 'The cherry orchard will be coming up for sale on the twenty-second of August'. Each actor pursued his activity, but whenever he came into contact with another actor he would speak one of his chosen lines and receive another line in return, or vice versa.

When the whole thing was set in motion, it was amazing how energised and self-perpetuating it quickly became. It was important for the actors to remain on support and to be physically responsive, maintaining the activities on a slightly heightened level, so that, freed from all the constraints of the performance context, they could create all sorts of physical situations and new contexts for speaking their phrases. Since they were already clear about the identities of the other characters and the basic relationships, they were then able to discover all sorts of new things about both the world of the play and their own character's attitude towards the other characters.

Within this context it is then possible for small groups of actors within the ensemble to play their specific scenes. As long as the actors are open and responsive to what is going on around them and not determined to cling to a fixed interpretation, two things can happen. Firstly they can experience the world of the play in the fullest sense, allowing themselves to be emotionally affected, not just by words and situations but by the whole heady atmosphere of the space.

And secondly they can start to observe the nature of this world and the characters within it, thereby gaining a clearer sense of the relationships and the obstacles within that world. What is very important is that the actor can and should, in the words of David Mamet, 'Deny nothing, invent nothing, accept everything.'[19] Everything that happens in the space, whether within the scene or just part of the ensemble, must be noticed and allowed to shape the way the lines are spoken. Nothing needs to be invented because all the stimuli the actor needs will be there in the space.

Actors who have done this exercise have often observed afterwards that its strength lies in the fact that it serves both as a physical improvisation game which helps them set up the world of the play with all its rhythms and atmospheres, and also as a painless method for making the text active and dynamic without having to force anything. The text is introduced to the improvised world in a flexible and malleable way, allowing the actors to experience not its strictures and 'other-ness', but its power and effectiveness in a series of actual contexts. The situations created by the interaction of all these underlying activities allow the actors to make discoveries about the world of the play and their character's relationships which are absolutely specific to *this* company of actors, *this* space and *this* moment.

The name I give to exercises of this nature is 'defamiliarisation exercises' – in other words, techniques for preventing you from speaking and gesturing the text in fixed ways which with each successive rehearsal become more engrained and less open to change.

TRANSACTIONAL ANALYSIS

Another such exercise, which also compels the actor to make very different physical and vocal offers, is derived from Transactional Analysis.

This is a term coined by the psychologist Eric Berne. It is used in therapy and counselling to help define and work through the strategies employed by individuals in different situations. One of its most important principles is the idea that we do not have a single 'personality', but employ different roles to fit different situations and encounters. Transactional Analysis broadly defines these 'ego-states' as 'child', 'parent', and 'adult', and observes that they are not the conscious strategies of a single personality, but separate personalities, each with its own pattern of thought and feeling, which we switch in and out of in response to outside stimuli.

If we stop to think about it, we have all at some point employed these roles in our everyday lives. Mature professionals in their forties can quite easily slip into child mode if their boss is over-parental, and within that mode can be either emotional and dependent or rebellious and irrational, according to the situation. Primary school teachers might perhaps be so used to being in parent mode within their school and home lives that they find it hard to move into adult or child where other situations demand.

Broadly, the 'parent' role can be defined as *corrective, protective* and *educative*; the 'child' role as *irrational, vulnerable, emotional* and *rebellious*; and the 'adult' role as *rational, self-aware* and *negotiative*. For the purposes of actor training I have also added a sub-division of adult, which we call 'Lover'. Lover is *sexual, flirtatious* and *intense*, but also assumes adult equality and does not try to enact parent or child roles within a sexual situation. It is also not necessarily physical.

For you to take on a transactional role of this kind, while performing a scene with another actor, requires only that you allow everything that you say and do to be conditioned by your awareness of the boundaries and demands of the predetermined relationship. This is not something you need to think about or consciously demonstrate in each moment, because once the opening offers have been made and responded to, the relationship will become self-sustaining.

Within the actor's process, as in real life, there are certain combinations of roles which can be described as 'stable' in the sense that two actors can sustain these roles through a lengthy improvisation or scene with each other. There are others which are unsustainable and must quickly transform into a different combination if there is to be any transactional gain on either side.

The most obvious sustainable combination is *parent-child* or *child-parent*. Assuming that each actor is happy with their role, this can be sustained almost indefinitely, since the more the 'child' is childish, the more the 'parent' will seek to be parental and vice versa. In real life two grown people can easily fall into a *parent-child* relationship, although this will normally require some kind of set status relationship to ensure its continuing viability, such as professional ranking or age difference. A marriage partnership might also use this combination from time to time, although the partners will usually switch roles according to the context. So, for example, one partner might become the parent in order to 'correct' the other's dress-sense, whereas in a different context (filling in the tax-return), the roles might be reversed.

The second stable combination is of course *adult-adult*. This tends to operate outside families in professional or social situations. It is common in the workplace, or among groups of friends, and while it can at times of need give way to parent-child on a temporary basis where one person has a crisis and needs nurture from a friend, adult-adult tends to re-establish itself in these situations as soon as possible. Here, unlike the parent-child combinations which can exist outside the family, there is no fixed status relationship to define the roles played, which allows for more adaptability. In other words, where a relationship is assumed to be one of equals, it can employ any stable combination as appropriate.

Lover-lover is also potentially stable, although it also has the capacity to change into other combinations and back again. Most healthy sexual relationships start with the assumption of this version of adult-adult, and will keep this at their base. Sexual relationships which have their root in parent-child or child-parent will tend ultimately to fail, since the sexuality which derives from such combinations tends to be a transitional stage for the 'child' partner from which they will eventually move on.

Other combinations are inherently unstable, and will neither last long nor lead to a productive outcome. These include *adult-child*, where the adult becomes increasingly perplexed with the child's refusal to be an adult and the child frustrated at not getting its parental 'fix'. This combination will usually quickly become either parent-child, as the adult's irritation shifts her into parent mode, or adult-adult, as the child realises that his strategies are not working and abandons them.

Another unsuccessful combination is *child-child*. When we see actual children playing, we should not assume that in the terms of Transactional Analysis they are in the roles of child-child, no matter how childish their behaviour may appear to us. Most children when playing with each other will be using either adult-adult or parent-child combinations. The moment both start using child a conflict situation will arise, and one or both children will then immediately go and seek a parent figure. Very often, older and younger children will find it hard to play together, since their differing age and experience makes adult-adult hard to achieve, and both children may for different reasons resent having the parent-child roles forced upon them; the older because she does not want to give up the child role herself, the younger because he does not want the older child to have the status and determining power of the parent.

Combinations such as *adult-parent* and *parent-parent* are also unstable, for obvious reasons, and will either speedily transform into stable combinations or else the parties will disengage from each other and terminate the exchange.

It is possible for you to use transactional ego-states, not as a form of self analysis, but as a way of approaching your interactions, within both improvised and text-based forms of repetition. They can also be employed to inform character archetypes. In the case of improvised repetition this is merely a way of redefining the transaction between two actors who perhaps find it hard to break out of their 'real-life' relationship within the group. In much the same way, you can apply the ego-states to text in order to challenge the assumptions which you might have made about the play and the characters.

The David Mamet play *Oleanna* deals with the thorny relationship between John, a paternalistic university professor, and Carol, a frustrated female student. One might be inclined to see the relationship between John and Carol as a classic example of parent-child. However, it is possible for the actors to reverse these roles to child-parent, or instead to play lover-lover, in order to avoid getting stuck in parent-child. To do this, the actors have only to allow themselves to change the way they view each other, seeing through the 'lens' of their altered ego-state, just as they do when they see through the 'lens' of their archetype. Take for example the following exchange from Act 1 of the play:

CAROL. Why did you stay here with me?

JOHN. Stay here.

CAROL. Yes. When you should have gone.

JOHN. Because I like you.

Using text repetition the actors create a longer exchange, with Carol as parent and John as child:

CAROL *(as parent)*. Why did you stay here with me?

JOHN *(as child)*. Why did I stay here with you?

CAROL. Why did you stay here with me?

JOHN. Why did I stay here with you?

CAROL. Why did you stay here with me?

JOHN. Stay here.

CAROL. Stay here.

JOHN. Stay here.

CAROL. Stay here.

JOHN. Stay here.

CAROL. Yes. When you should have gone.

JOHN. When I should have gone.

CAROL. When you should have gone.

JOHN. When I should have gone.

CAROL. When you should have gone.

JOHN. Because I like you.

CAROL. Because you like me.

It is easy to assume that this exchange is between a vulnerable student looking for reassurance and a powerful male authority figure taking advantage of this to shift the relationship from a professional onto a personal level. Without *denying* this analysis, it is useful for actors in rehearsal to explore its antithesis, so they can expose further the complexity of the game-playing which goes on between John and Carol. If in the above fragment Carol is the parent and John the child then what is exposed is her awareness of professional irregularity, and his neediness, which creates a very different dynamic. It should be stressed once again this is not an *interpretation*; it is a level of exploration which the actors need to undertake in order to experience the possibilities within this relationship.

The other combination which the actors could try out is lover-lover. In this case the text becomes an elaborate game in which the political power and authority conferred upon the characters by the *institution* at each point in the play negotiates with the sexual power each generates in the space. Let's reiterate that this is not an attempt to find a definitive new interpretation of the play, it is an exercise for exploring the ways in which the actors playing these roles can exert power. Mamet's play is neither radically feminist nor misogynist – it deals with the contradictions and complexities which can arise when political ideology collides with human vulnerabilities. It is a play which demands that the actors work from their own needs and sensibilities in the space, and confront the politics from within that world rather than from outside it.

Defamiliarisation exercises serve not only to lift you out of your 'rut' and prevent you from speaking your lines in exactly the same way each time, but also to overturn your preconceptions about the play you are working on. Whenever we read a play or begin work on a character we have a tendency to file these away in some sort of mental pigeon-hole. These pigeonholes are attached to what are loosely termed the 'grand narratives' of our cultural tradition. So, for instance, we might file *Hedda Gabler* under human tragedy, *Loot* under black farce and *Top Girls* under feminist theatre. Unfortunately, such labels can be reductive and limiting. It is your job when 'playing around' to try and forget the label and, without ignoring the play's social and historical context, to see if it can be played in other ways or in other styles, and what emerges if you do.

What does emerge is always useful and often unexpected. I have asked actors to sing the lines of *A Doll's House* to each other like opera singers, and in doing so they have suddenly realised which are the most significant or emotive phrases in the text and given these appropriate weight. Through the sung word they have also found a stronger connection between words and the movement of the body in space. I have asked actors rehearsing *The Crucible* to do scenes as if they were characters from *The Simpsons,* and they discovered a neurotic energy and grotesque quality which they had never found before and which made a strong link between seventeenth-century America and present-day America. I have asked actors rehearsing Dürrenmatt's *The Visit* to play the text in Deep South accents, and they have discovered a brooding fear and a sense of abandonment and alienation in the town. To remove a play from its supposed genre and cultural context and apply different codings to it in rehearsal is to allow actors to make new connections and access knowledge and cultural references which are stored away in their experience but which they might not have brought to bear on this particular play. Merely to discuss these ideas is not enough – a company of actors needs literally to play with them, to try them out, so the experience of relating to each other on text in a new and unexpected way can form part of the 'layering' of a rehearsal process.

Defamiliarisation can take place early in rehearsal as a way of getting the text off the page and into the space, or it can be introduced at a later stage of rehearsal to prevent you from fixing your performance or becoming set in your ways. Other such exercises include:

The 'Stop' Exercise

Actor 1 speaks a line to Actor 2, and Actor 2 calls out 'stop!' when he hears a key word (trigger word) or phrase which he feels he needs to respond to. He then immediately speaks his response line, and Actor 1 calls out 'stop!' for the same reason. However, if the 'stop!' comes a long way from the end of the speech, Actor 2 might decide she needs to finish the speech, and override the interruption.

This will make Actor 1 desperate to speak, and so the energy and pace of the exchange is heightened. We also get rid of the 'polite' style of acting in which you wait patiently for each other to finish a line before starting to respond.

The following passage is taken from Act 3 of *Oleanna*.

CAROL. You tried to rape me. (*Pause.*) According to the law. (*Pause.*)

JOHN. . . . what . . . ?

CAROL. You tried to rape me. I was leaving this office, you 'pressed' yourself into me. You 'pressed' your body into me

JOHN. . . . I . . .

CAROL. My group has told your lawyer that we may pursue criminal charges.

JOHN. . . . no . . .

Using the 'stop' exercise, you might deliver this exchange as follows:

CAROL. You tried to rape me.

JOHN. Stop!

CAROL (*overrides him*). According to the law.

JOHN. Stop! . . . what . . . ?

CAROL. Stop! You tried to rape me. I was leaving this office, you 'pressed' yourself into me . . .

JOHN. Stop!

CAROL (*overrides him*). You 'pressed' your body into . . .

JOHN. Stop! . . . I . . .

CAROL. Stop! My group has told your lawyer that we may pursue criminal charges.

JOHN. Stop! . . . no . . .

The 'stop' exercise makes you listen more carefully to each other, and also makes you aware of the need for you to intervene actively in the conversation, which in this case is being driven by Carol towards a disastrous place for John. On the other hand Carol cannot afford to let John speak, because her assertions are vulnerable to being overturned by John's rhetoric. The 'stops' help you discover or rediscover the urgency within the conflict and prevent it from becoming ritualised as a result of your over-familiarity with the scene.

It is worth mentioning at this point that Mamet has professed himself scornful of actor exercises which add words or phrases to the author's text, seeing them as self-indulgent and meaningless. He quotes an exercise in *True and False* where actors add the phrase 'I mean' to the beginning of each line to make them feel they own the line. However, it should be understood the 'I mean' exercise is the exact opposite to the 'stop!' exercise in that it makes the actor inward-looking and de-energises the text. The 'stop!' exercise, by contrast, is active, outwardly directed and re-energising. It does not necessarily work for every speech and every piece of text, but then, like any rehearsal exercise, it is not an end in itself.

The 'Touch' Exercise

Another version of the 'stop!' exercise is the 'touch' exercise, where instead of calling out 'stop' you physically touch the other actor before you speak your line. The nature of the touch is found in the moment – it might be aggressive, gentle, consoling, sexual or whatever. It might be on the hand, face, shoulder, knee or any other part of the body. The important thing is that the touch and the next line should not happen simultaneously; instead the next line should be influenced by the experience of the touch.

In a scene like the one above, which is actually about the meaning of physical touching, using the touching exercise can be quite electrifying, especially as John does not seem able at this point to express himself verbally. Just as the 'stop!' exercise allows the actors to intervene verbally in the space, so the touch exercise allows them to affect each other physically.

It is possible, however, for the touch to become sidelined and mechanical, particularly if you are anticipating it and trying to make it interesting for those watching. To avoid this, the touch must happen on the out-breath so that it connects with a physical impulse and initiates from your centre. In this way the touch can have a direct effect on how the text is spoken.

It is important when doing defamiliarisation exercises that you do not allow the rules of the exercise to stop you watching, listening and responding to one another. If the demonstration of 'doing the exercise' itself becomes the priority then the text itself will be sidelined. As with so many aspects of actor training, breathing is the key to maintaining the direct and unforced connection between your experience in the space and the vocal choices you make on the text.

'Playing around' is a crucial part of your rehearsal process. Most good directors could probably add to this chapter at least another half-dozen techniques for working on text in a way that engages the actor in the space and allows them to *use* the text rather than dutifully to *deliver* it. But the act of playing in this sense has a deeper significance. Actors who genuinely engage with each other through structured exercises, including the repetition exercises, will achieve the same effect as any other group of people who 'play' together, which is a genuine social bonding, based on observation and knowledge of each other, and more particularly on the fact that at times they will have been exposed and vulnerable in the space. A rehearsal process in which you merely present carefully prepared work over which you have complete control will be a very impersonal experience, even if the play is full of emotion. It will also create a company of actors who are curiously disengaged from one another, and this will show in performance.

Actors are like anyone else – you will engage with others and reveal yourselves only when you feel safe to do so, and that safety is only achieved through the experience of seeing others reveal and engage. Any company of actors will ultimately be exposed to the scrutiny of many strangers in the audience; long before that happens it is essential for you to feel that you can be vulnerable with each other – that beneath everything you have the support of the social unit which is the company. Audiences can sense whether a group of actors are genuinely open to one another, and it is only when they detect a chemistry, a shared history and the actors' ability to affect one another, that an audience will really start to watch.

15

Subtext

There has been much sense and nonsense talked about subtext in plays – what it is, how one reveals it, whether the actor should even think about it or just leave it to chance. There are many possible definitions of subtext, but a good simple definition for the actor might be 'meanings which may be conveyed by a line of text, which go beyond the surface meaning of the words'.

David Mamet might claim that the whole notion of subtext is a nonsense and an irrelevance, and that you should get on with speaking the text, not worrying about the subtext. To an extent, of course, he would be right. In the moment of performance you should not be concentrating on delivering meanings which you have previously read into the text. Having said that, where the text is complex and constructed with different layers of meaning, you will need to have explored these thoroughly in rehearsal, otherwise you risk under-serving the text and failing to reveal the subtext. The process of 'gaining ownership' of the text is one of exploration and revelation, and there is some text, including some of Mamet's own, where it is hard to see on first or even second reading either why the playwright has given a character this particular speech in this context, or what, within this context, the speech might mean. You may have a vague idea, but a vague idea is not enough. Playwrights write specific words, not vague approximations, and even if the playwright is not available for comment, you have a duty to come into the space with clear offers on the text, even if these change radically during the rehearsal process. You must acknowledge and take on board this responsibility at an early stage, otherwise the text in rehearsal will quickly descend into a depressing catalogue of vague or incomprehensible exchanges, which offer nothing and demand nothing. If your main aim in rehearsal is to respond to one another, this can be utterly frustrating and demoralising.

Much of the text written nowadays is fairly explicit, and you will probably have little difficulty getting to grips with it, in the sense that you will be able to see how the text reveals the action both in its general direction and in the specifics of each word and phrase. However, not all text offers this level of transparency. Some authors put words into the mouths of their characters which actors puzzle over, unsure about why the character is saying a line, and equally unsure about how the line connects to the last one. Chekhov, Wedekind, Brecht, Beckett, Pinter, Churchill, Wertenbaker, Edgar, Bond, Rudkin and Kane, to name but a few, are all playwrights whose texts are at times challenging for the actor when she comes to ask the most basic questions of 'why is my character saying this line?' or 'why do the stage directions tell my character to perform this action?'

Few playwrights ever comment on the specifics of their work. Some demand absolute fidelity to the last pause or semi-colon, while others are less pedantic, but hardly any offer the actor or director more than just the text itself. What this means is the task of getting the play into the space in a comprehensible form is usually the sole responsibility of the acting company, and to some extent of the individual actor. Complex dramatic text is invariably working on many levels. It may contain metaphors, political allegory and non-verbal action placed in juxtaposition to the words themselves. It may also be seeking to challenge the conventions of realist dialogue, linear narrative and coherent characterisations. A company of actors may have to work very hard to discover what a text offers and to find ways of conveying those meanings to an audience.

Any company working on a complex text will spend significant amounts of time exploring meanings, a process sometimes called 'interrogating the text', which can take place via discussion and through working the text in the space. In addition, the company may place new interpretations or 'readings' on the text and find ways of conveying these through the staging. The extent to which the actor is involved in this dramaturgical process will depend on the director and the company she is working for, and on how the director sees the play and the process through which it will be realised. However, in any dramatic text which uses dialogue to sign interactive exchanges between recognisable social beings within specific situations, even if these are non-linear and non-realist, the actor will always have to address the basic questions relating to these exchanges, and ultimately will have to find a way of engaging cognitively and emotionally with other actors as fully as if she were performing in a well-made three-act play. If a playwright has written dialogue then the actors need to make sense of that dialogue, so the audience can find recognition.

Sense and recognition will almost invariably include an element of human interest and dramatic tension. An audience whose attention is gripped by an exchange, however brief, will be interested on an emotional and empathetic as well as an intellectual level in the processes and outcomes of that interaction, provided, that is, they believe in what the actors are doing. A play which, in seeking to challenge convention, only succeeds in confusing and alienating its audience, will fail on all levels, because for a play to be challenging it must first engage its audience emotionally. Meanings and ideas alone are not enough – there has to be human interest. Where the playwright has not made clear the nature of the interaction between the characters in an emotional sense, it is the actors' job to discover this, so that the audience will be able to understand the performance on the level of emotional transactions as well as intellectually.

In other words, whatever the play, its political message, radical form or verbal complexity, your main task is *to make your scenes make sense*, firstly by making some clear initial choices about the meaning of the text and secondly by going into the rehearsal space to find out why this character speaks those words at that time in that place to that other character, and what the consequences of this might be. Within this process there is a limit to what you can discover on your

own. The key to realising any scene has to be the application
of the text to the living dynamic of actors in the space. Before
that process begins, however, there are certain techniques
which you can apply to the interpretation of text, which can
then be taken into the space and used as a starting point for
exploring the scene.

SUBTEXTUAL COMMENTS

The first principle the actor needs to apply to any dialogue
scene is that whenever one character speaks to another, even
if she is talking about something or someone outside the
scene, there is always a *subtextual comment* being made *to*
and *about* the person who is actually present. This is a vitally
important principle for discovering and keeping alive the
dramatic tension and dynamic between the actors in the
space. In Chekhov's plays, for instance, it often appears that
the characters are drifting off into nostalgic or idealistic
dream-worlds, making long speeches which no-one really
listens to and which don't relate particularly to the immediate surroundings of the speaker. To interpret the plays only
on this level is to turn them into rather dreary pieces of
wistful nostalgia, which although we can perhaps relate to it
empathetically in terms of our own sense of loss and regret,
is unfortunately not enough to sustain us through all four
acts of a full-length Chekhov drama. Although a lover of
Chekhov, I have often found myself stifled by the tedium of
watching actors performing in bubbles. It is easy to see why
actors and directors misinterpret Chekhov in this way. Olga's
opening speech in Act 1 of his *Three Sisters*, for example,
seems to set the tone of the play as a piece in which the
characters all sit around mourning a lost past and fantasising
about a bright future which is clearly never going to arrive.
Yet what if the actor chooses to read this speech differently?
True, Olga is talking about the past, but she is talking *to* and
therefore *about* her sister Irina. If one takes each phrase or
section of the speech and asks the question 'what is Olga
saying to and about Irina with this section?' then one arrives
at the *subtextual comment* – the underlying reason for making the speech in that place, at that time, to that person,

through which the actor can then begin to discover the dynamic of the scene.

Olga's first comment is: '*Father died exactly a year ago, this very day. On your name-day, Irina, the fifth of May.*' What exactly is her reason for saying this? We don't doubt the accuracy of her facts, but why on earth would she need to remind her sister of something Irina already knows, especially as the anniversary of their father's death has probably already been mentioned that day? Olga's reason must lie in that moment and in the dynamic of her relationship with Irina. Other parts of the scene suggest that Olga feels old and unattractive, that she is jealous of her sisters' looks, that she misses her father's love, that possibly she felt herself to be his favourite child. It is also clear that Irina has fonder memories of her mother than of her father. Suppose, then, that Olga's subtextual comment to Irina is '*You've forgotten father*' or even '*You never really loved father*'. Suddenly the opening line of this speech is not wistful or nostalgic – it is a strong and biting reproach which expresses not past dreams but very present issues of sibling rivalry and jealousy. Olga continues: 'It was very cold then –snowing. I thought I'd never get over it, and you had fainted, lying as if you were dead'. On the face of it this is a mere reliving of a poignant and difficult experience which the two of them shared, but what if Olga is really saying '*I suffered in silence and you got all the attention*'? Suddenly this is a play steeped in bitterness, hatred and desire. The audience can look up from their programmes and realise that far from being in for three hours of wistful inaction, they are sitting on the edge of a battlefield. The speech continues: 'And here we are, a year's gone by, and we can talk about it quite calmly.' Again, this could be just an innocent statement, or it could mask yet another subtextual comment, this time along the lines of '*You're callous*' or '*You don't care*'.

To find the subtextual comments all the actor has to do is look at the literal meaning of the text and ask herself what that literal meaning *might* be saying about the person to whom the text is addressed. To do this an actor needs an excellent working knowledge of the play, including, where appropriate, the family relationships, the social structure and the background facts as we know them. In Act 4 Masha, who is mourning the impending departure of her lover Vershinin, approaches the elderly doctor Chebutykin and asks him 'Were you in love with my mother?' Of course, Masha could be just looking for a kindred spirit to empathise with her hopeless passion for a married man. But what if this is a statement of quite a different kind? The play is full of extra-marital affairs – Natasha with Protopopov, Masha with Vershinin, so why shouldn't Masha's subtextual comment to Chebutykin be '*You're my father*' – not a question but a statement. The issue here is not whether Chebutykin is or isn't Masha's biological father – we could never know for sure one way or the other. The point is that Masha might *suspect* it and that Chebutykin might know she suspects it, and by playing around with the subtextual comments the two of them can create a level of dramatic tension which the scene otherwise lacks. It is important that the actor does not see the subtextual comments as fixed secret codes which the playwright has hidden for her to discover. The subtextual comments are not hidden truths, they are ways of getting the actors to engage with each other in a purposeful and mean-ingful way even when the text itself suggests a rather desul-tory or distracted quality to the relationship, or where the immediate relevance of the dialogue is not particularly clear.

The best way to identify the subtextual comments is for the actors in a scene to work together in close discussion. Once they have identified the underlying issues within a scene and between characters, such as the class gap between Olga and Natasha at the start of Act 3, it is not hard to see how the characters pursue their agendas via the subtextual comments. Most actors I have worked with in this way are amazed at the level of emotion and often hatred they un-cover. Behind the apparent formality in Chekhov, or the characters' baffling and obscure role-play in the works of Harold Pinter you can find fear and desire at a level which you would never have suspected from the text alone. By starting from the assumption that every line of dialogue a character utters is stimulated by the significant presence of another character, you can find the key to creating a strong dynamic with each other which will ultimately cause the text to resonate far more dangerously in the space.

[177]

Pinter's *The Birthday Party* is about the character Stanley who lives in a run-down seaside boarding house. At first glance, this breakfast-time exchange between Stanley and Meg the landlady seems like a kind of ritualised game, in which Stanley teasingly criticises Meg about her housekeeping skills, and Meg responds defensively:

STANLEY. You're a bad wife.

MEG. I'm not. Who said I am?

STANLEY. Not to make your husband a cup of tea. Terrible.

MEG. He knows I'm not a bad wife.

STANLEY. Giving him sour milk instead.

MEG. It wasn't sour.

STANLEY. Disgraceful.

MEG. You mind your own business anyway. (*Stanley eats.*) You won't find many better wives than me, I can tell you. I keep a very nice house and I keep it clean.

STANLEY. Whoo!

The dialogue is clearly not supposed to be played as a turning-point or especially significant event within the characters' relationship, yet neither should it come across as too benign, since it prefigures the hidden menace of the play's later events. Identifying possible subtextual comments can help the actors find the underlying transaction in this exchange. The subtextual comments printed in bold below are merely suggestions, which the actors might start with, but which at any time they could decide to change.

STANLEY. You're a bad wife. (*You're not giving me what I need.*)

MEG. I'm not. Who said I am? (*You don't respect me.*)

STANLEY. Not to make your husband a cup of tea. Terrible. (*You neglect me.*)

MEG. He knows I'm not a bad wife. (*You think I'm old and ugly.*)

STANLEY. Giving him sour milk instead. (*You've let yourself go.*)

MEG. It wasn't sour. (*You're very cruel.*)

STANLEY. Disgraceful. (*You flaunt yourself.*)

MEG. You mind your own business anyway. (*Stanley eats.*) You won't find many better wives than me, I can tell you. I keep a very nice house and I keep it clean. (*You've got a filthy bloody mind!.*)

STANLEY. Whoo! (*You're in denial!.*)

The subtextual comments in this case reveal an intimacy and co-dependency between these two characters, so that, even though Stanley is ostensibly commenting on Meg's treatment of her husband Petey, subtextually he could actually be commenting on the frustrations of his own relationship with her. Later in the scene it becomes even clearer that there is a sexual subtext between Stanley and Meg, and there is also a series of status games, through which they both struggle to raise their self-esteem by dominating or criticising each other. The purpose of these subtextual comments is to give the actors working on the scene a fuller sense of the characters' underlying need for one another than the text itself might offer. The nature of the statements is also very emotive, allowing the actors to experience the emotions which underscore the dialogue.

USING THE SUBTEXTUAL COMMENTS

Between identifying the subtextual comments and working with the text in the space, however, there are several further stages to this process. It is not enough for you to have an idea of a possible subtext and to speak the actual text with that in mind. You need to experience, in the space and in your body, the extremes of your relationships with the other actors, so that when you eventually speak the text, you will do so with a strong physical sense of what you are saying. To begin with, the actors in the scene simply need to sit opposite one another and speak the subtextual comments aloud to each other without the text itself, and to create a new *subtextual dialogue*. This is partly so you can familiarise yourselves with the statements and partly to make the statements flow naturally from one another as spontaneous reactions, as one might attempt to do with any text. At this stage it should become clear, especially with the rest of the company observing, if any of the subtextual comments is not quite right, or does not seem to fit with the rest, in which case it can be changed by common consent.

The next stage is to use the subtextual comments for *text repetition*, as described in Chapter 13:

STANLEY. You're not giving me what I need.

MEG. I'm not giving you what you need.

STANLEY. You're not giving me what I need.

MEG. You don't respect me.

STANLEY. I don't respect you.

MEG. You don't respect me.

STANLEY. You neglect me.

MEG. I neglect you.

STANLEY. You neglect me.

MEG. I neglect you ...You think I'm old and ugly.

STANLEY. I think you're old and ugly.

MEG. You think I'm old and ugly.

STANLEY. I think you're old and ugly.

MEG. You think I'm old and ugly.

STANLEY. You've let yourself go.

MEG. I've let myself go.

STANLEY. You've let yourself go.

MEG. You're very cruel ...

And so on. By forcing you to repeat back the comments made about you, the exercise prevents the exchange being purely antagonistic, demanding that you recognise and submit to the comments, even if you find them difficult. The continued repetition means that even if you resist submitting to a comment, you will eventually give in.

The next stage is to repeat the last exercise, but this time responding to physical impulses stimulated by both text and the other actors, allowing yourself full physical permission within the space. The effects of this are usually startling. The combination of the direct and uncensored statements together with direct and uncensored physical responses creates a level of focus and emotional openness which the text alone would have been unlikely to generate. Freed from what you perceive to be the formality of the text and the period, you can find ownership of the comments and of the space.

Finally you return to the real text, still flushed from your physical experiences in the space, and very aware of the hidden agendas and suppressed emotions in the scene. And suddenly the text resonates. It stops being dull dreamy nostalgia and becomes alive, fast, full of energy and above all, about *now*. From the moment Stanley speaks we understand how frustrated and disappointed he is, with his life and his breakfast, and how far he is prepared to take his frustration out on Meg, by taunting her with her low self-esteem and repressed sexuality. The audience can now feel they are observing, not just a tedious daily ritual, but two people locked into a mutually-dependent yet abusive relationship.

By the time you step into the performance space the subtextual comments may have changed several times, but that is not important. You do not need to retain them in your conscious mind, because you have already experienced them in the fullest sense in the space, and they have become part of your understanding of the text whether you like it or not! Back within the more concrete world of Pinter's seaside town or Chekhov's Russia you are free, within the parameters of these worlds, to play with the text. All you have to do is remain aware that everything you say will affect others; everything they say will affect you. Change will happen.

I cannot recommend this exercise highly enough to the actor. In its various stages it serves the rehearsal process in many different ways. It encourages you to think the unthinkable about your character and their relationship with others; it asks you to see character in terms of the extremes of human fear and desire; it engages you with each other on a physical, intellectual and emotional level. It creates energy and dynamics within the scene. Provided the subtextual comments are sourced intelligently and with due regard for the information in the text, they will ultimately serve the play and help you to understand it afresh.

One thing which you need to become aware of is that actors read texts differently from everyone else. It is fine and necessary to research around a text; it is good for you to be involved in dramaturgy and to understand performance in its widest sense. But for all that, for you the text is first and foremost a doorway into something alive and very personal – a set of signposts pointing you towards actual physical and emotional experiences which you must undergo in order to do your job. Physicalising and vocalising the subtext is one way for you to find the rawness and immediacy of plays whose language may be repressed and formal but whose underlying passions must become real and visceral in the space.

16

Shakespeare and the Actor

Most drama schools devote a considerable amount of teaching and rehearsal time training their actors to work on Shakespeare's texts. While Shakespeare continues to be the western world's best known and most performed playwright, it is not just for this reason that these texts are seen as such important building blocks in the actor's development. For many professional actors, drama school will be their first and last experience of actually performing Shakespeare, yet the experience of learning how to unlock these texts is still of immense value to you in terms of your general development, confidence and self-empowerment, for reasons I shall attempt to make clear in this chapter. While there is a limit to the ground that can be covered by one chapter on so vast a subject, I hope that this chapter will help you to see Shakespeare in a different light and suggest some new approaches to his text.

One of the features of Shakespeare's plays which makes them so attractive to the actor is that they are not 'over-written'. In other words, while the texts offer a myriad of opportunities and instructions to the actor through their use of language and rhythm, the intensity of the drama, and the struggles and dilemmas of the characters, Shakespeare does not appear to be especially interested in the 'well-made play', nor in psychologically-rounded characters. Much of what his characters actually do is quite puzzling. Characters fall in love at first sight (often with cross-dressers), change their minds, give away their kingdoms and construct elaborate plots against one another, often with fairly flimsy motivations.

Usually we are asked to accept their stated reasons at face value, but it is sometimes hard to believe that these alone could be sufficient motivation for what follows. For this reason simply reading Shakespeare's plays without working them in the space can be a baffling and frustrating experience. Like most plays, they were written to be performed, and the logic of the characters' actions can only be revealed through the actors' real and visible transactions with each other in a living context. Furthermore we have to remember that what the audience sees and understands is not the truth of the play, but the truth of a particular performance within a particular production. For the actor there can be no other truth.

The language of Shakespeare differs from that of the realist traditions in the sense that it never pretends to be 'real' speech. In Shakespeare's time theatre was self-consciously theatre. It produced its own conventions, language and sign-systems, which had a relationship with the real world but did not claim to be one with it. The language itself is highly explicit. There are no 'whodunnits' in Shakespeare, because the villainy of Shakespearean villains is revealed to the audience from the outset, usually by the villain himself. Every subterfuge, every deception practised is announced to us before it happens. The audience has an omniscient position from start to finish, overhearing in soliloquy the innermost thoughts of the characters framed in language of startling candour and clarity. Shakespeare's dramas are heightened and distilled reflections of complex social and personal interactions, yet the characters as written are not psychologically complex in a modern sense. A speech or scene which signs a character in dilemma may vividly reveal to us the contradictions of that dilemma through the ideas, texture and rhythm of the language, but it will not attempt through that language to indicate any deeper motivations or hidden psychological processes which lie outside of the character's knowledge and control. For this reason Shakespeare sits uneasily within the realist humanist tradition. There is no subtext to this language in the sense that one might find it in Ibsen or Chekhov; the thought-processes are laid out within the text itself, and any attempt to impose subtextual meanings is likely to disrupt the flow and rhythm of the text and thereby blur the clarity of the language. One should remember that this text was not written in the age of darkened theatres and silent audiences, or of camera close-ups capturing every eyebrow flicker. The precision and weight of each thought and its juxtaposition with the next, possibly antithetical, thought, depended on the actor's ability to deliver the text according to the rhythm of the line and with due regard to the pace, pitch and intonation suggested by the phonic relationship of each sound to the line's overall meaning and emotional quality. A series of hard 'guttural', 'fricative' and 'plosive' consonants and short vowel sounds placed in quick succession within a line expressing anger, for example, may be telling the actor that this particular line should be delivered like a burst of machine-gun fire or a series of verbal blows:

MARGARET
   Poor painted queen, vain flourish of my fortune:
   Why strew'st thou sugar on that bottled spider?
   Fool, fool; thou whet'st a knife to kill thyself.
   The day will come that thou shalt wish for me
   To help thee curse this poisonous bunch-back'd toad.[20]

A series of soft 'fricative' and 'sibilant' consonants accompanied by longer vowel sounds, on the other hand, might suggest a slower and more measured form of attack, using a different pitch and tone.

RICHARD
   More wonderful, when angels are so angry.
   Vouchsafe, divine perfection of a woman,
   Of these supposed crimes, to give me leave,
   By circumstance, but to acquit myself.[21]

At the same time a line which adheres strictly to the iambic metre might indicate compliance or self-control, while a line which breaks the metrical rules could signal (according to the context) rebellion, emotion or confusion. Compare these two speeches from *Twelfth Night*. The first is a courtly expression of love, which obeys conventions both of language, and, for the most part, of metre. This is an emotion over which the speaker has full control:

ORSINO

> O, she that hath a heart of that fine frame
> To pay this debt of love but to a brother,
> How will she love, when the rich golden shaft
> Hath kill'd the flock of all affections else
> That live in her; when liver, brain and heart,
> These sovereign thrones, are all supplied and fill'd
> Her sweet perfections with one self king!
> Away before me to sweet beds of flowers!
> Love-thoughts lie rich when canopied with bowers.[22]

The second speech, from later in the play, when Olivia is revealing her love to Cesario, stands in stark contrast to the first example. Here the metre begins conventionally, but is increasingly disrupted, revealing Olivia's wilder and more desperate state of mind:

OLIVIA

> Give me leave, beseech you. I did send,
> After the last enchantment you did here,
> A ring in chase of you. So did I abuse
> Myself, my servant, and, I fear me, you.
> Under your hard construction must I sit,
> To force that on you in a shameful cunning
> Which you knew none of yours. What might you think?
> Have you not set mine honour at the stake,
> And baited it with all th'unmuzzled thoughts
> That tyrannous heart can think? To one of your receiving
> Enough is shown; a cypress, not a bosom
> Hides my heart: so, let me hear you speak.[23]

In this way the language can not only inform the way the text is delivered, but also make very specific suggestions about your physical moves and gestures. A smooth and regular rhythm suggests a measured and calm way of moving; a disrupted rhythm suggests a more confused and agitated physicality.

All this is fertile ground for the actor. On the one hand there is the language, crafted and turned with such skill that the choice of words and images together with the 'heartbeat' rhythm of iambic pentameter offers you a comprehensive instruction on how to speak the text and therefore how to reveal its meaning. On the other hand there are a million and one unanswered questions about the characters' motivations, relationships, complexities and contradictions, which the text can help you to uncover, but only through practical working of the scenes in the space.

By following the clues contained in the text and trying out the language in the space, you will discover that, provided you have sufficient command of the words and rhythm, the text actually begins to 'direct' itself. Once you begin to work off one another, allowing the text to shape your thoughts and emotions, you will be amazed at how far the text reveals the action, not just emotionally but physically and psychologically too.

An awareness of how Shakespeare's language and rhythmic devices can shed light on the text can be of enormous assistance to actors who are puzzling over how to interpret a scene or part of a scene. The following is an example of simple clues in the text which when taken in combination with the actors' perceptions and impulses, lead them to a fuller understanding of a scene:

In Act 5 Scene 2 of *Othello*, after Desdemona has briefly revived and then died in Emilia's arms, there is a curious exchange between Othello and Emilia, in which she appears just for a few lines to accept that he is not guilty of Desdemona's murder.

OTHELLO. Why, how should she be murdered?

EMILIA. Alas, who knows?

OTHELLO. You heard her say herself it was not I.

EMILIA. She said so. I must needs report the truth.

It could be argued that this last line of Emilia's should be said with defiance, making it clear to Othello that she knows the truth and will shout it from the rooftops. However, the mild language and obedient rhythm of this line is curiously at odds with the language and rhythm of her furious condemnation of him a few lines later, where she employs potent images of devils and damnation and where extra syllables spill rebelliously out of the iambic metre. This interpretation would also make little sense of Othello's next line, in which he admits to the murder:

OTHELLO
She's like a liar gone to burning hell:
'Twas I that killed her.

There would be no need for Othello to make this confession if it were clear to him that Emilia was already convinced of his guilt. When I worked with a group of actors on the scene they were initially quite puzzled by this section, but we agreed that they should simply work within the context of the scene as a whole, impose nothing on the text and see what naturally arose. What they discovered was incredibly simple and logical. On raising her head from Desdemona's body, having realised she was dead, the actor playing Emilia suddenly realised she was in a room alone with a murderer and that he was between her and the door. From that point she began to play a game with him, to humour him, while trying to find an opportunity to make a dash for the door. The actor playing Othello immediately saw through the game, but chose to play with her like a cat plays with a mouse. At the point where she ran for the door and was about to escape, he pounced on her and forced her back into the room. His line, 'She's like a liar gone to burning hell' suddenly referred not just to Desdemona but to Emilia, and to all the lies and deception of Venetian women as he perceived them. As he took hold of her, the actor playing Emilia realised the futility of struggling, and submitted – at least physically – to his strength. Feeling she was going to suffer at his hands anyway, she had no need for caution, and she let fly with all the hatred and passion which she felt, not just about him, but about male power in general. Each line she spoke, because of the strength of the images and sounds, and because the rhythm was distorted with extra syllables, gave the actor playing Emilia more courage and permission to speak out of turn. Because of her physical predicament, she also felt the need to find a deeper sound, because although she couldn't physically oppose him, she still believed she could weaken him with words. A deeper sound meant more breath, and by taking this breath she both strengthened herself and made the actor playing Othello take a step back, giving room for the exchange of information which followed.

Of course this is not the only way to play this passage, and it would be unhelpful to imagine that Shakespeare has consciously or unconsciously written definitive instructions of this kind into the text. Shakespeare was acutely aware of the actor's art and his text was written not as a strait-jacket for you, but to equip you, through the language, with everything that you need to find your own way through the scene. Working with this text is a gift, because although you never have to lose touch with your own impulses or deny the truth of your own responses, the text will guide and steer you through the action on every level, from the intellectual and philosophical to the emotional and visceral. It achieves this, not by offering you rounded characters, or even well-structured storylines, but by the simple power of the exchanges taken one by one. The text affects both the speaker and the spoken to, so that provided you trust both the text and yourself in the space, you can find yourself going on an extraordinary journey, without needing to impose anything at all. The logic of Shakespeare's scenes does not emerge as a result of the actor 'colouring in' the subtext, but through the potent mixture of sound, meaning, rhythm and human impulse in the space. The living actor and the text complement and support each other in performance. Neither is more important than the other, and neither reaches its full potential without the other.

You should never try and force Shakespeare's text; rather you should trust it. The most useful thing you can do at home is to learn the text thoroughly, investigate the rhythm and find out what all the contemporary references mean. You can also usefully think about your 'offers', as described in Chapter 8, although it should be absolutely clear that these are only starting points which must remain open to change. What you should not do is try to build a character outside of the space or try, in isolation, to fill in background and detail for your character. To begin with it is enough to know the facts about the character as the text presents them. Whatever else you need to know you will discover in good time.

Although you may trust the text completely in each moment, when working on a whole play you may be confused by what appears to be a lack of regard for structure and consistency. While Shakespeare's plays usually work towards some kind of resolution, and while it is not unusual for a character to reach some kind of realisation or self-knowledge, this is far from being the rule. Storylines are often tied up without much regard for consistency of characterisation, and many supporting characters are left with their stories unresolved. *Twelfth Night, Measure for Measure,* and *Troilus and Cressida* are just three of the plays whose resolutions can leave us unconvinced.

Other plays can have us scratching our heads over the apparent lack of character 'through-line' from scene to scene. Katherine, in *The Taming of the Shrew,* goes from declaring she will never marry Petruchio in Act 2, to lamenting his failure to appear for the wedding in Act 3 Scene 2. The quickfire wit she displayed at their first meeting seems to have evaporated at the wedding feast, and by the time she arrives at Petruchio's house she has apparently become quite mild-mannered and parental in the face of his peevish outbursts. Although in Act 4 she briefly attacks Grumio, the servant, she gives Petruchio no more trouble beyond a few rather tearful appeals against his cruelty. True, the play is supposed to be about Katherine's 'taming', but it is hard to see just from the text how her spirit could be so easily broken, or why Petruchio feels he has to take the 'taming' process to these lengths.

In rehearsal, assuming two actors are working openly, using the text, and responding to one another in the moment, the logic and through-line of this relationship can begin to emerge. Again, this is not a matter of unearthing some hidden meaning; rather it is the simple reality of two actors communicating with each other, and using this text both to drive the action and to shape what is already there.

When I worked with a group of actors on this play, the two playing Petruchio and Katherine had already found a dynamic offstage which was not unlike that of Act 2 Scene 1 where the two characters first meet. The problem for the actor playing Katherine was how she could possibly ever truthfully submit to the actor playing Petruchio, since her view was that his ill-treatment of her could only ever make her angrier. We put aside this problem and concentrated on the early scenes. Eventually, through playing these scenes, the actor playing Katherine discovered that she enjoyed immensely having verbal sparring-matches with Petruchio, and that although part of her loathed his arrogance, another part was drawn to him as the only person in the play who could match her anarchic personality, who was not afraid of her and in addition actually seemed to like her and find her attractive. Together these actors found a sort of warring intimacy and *frisson* which then made perfect sense of Katherine's disappointment at his being late for the wedding. It became clear that the actor playing Katherine was looking forward to an exciting if stormy marriage, and believed that she would be a match for her Petruchio. The text suggests that the anarchy of the wedding ceremony does not upset her in the least, since she makes no comment on it on her arrival back home. The actor playing Katherine took this to mean that her character was in fact quite amused by Petruchio's flouting of convention, seeing him rather as a partner in rebellion than as part of a hostile system, and during Act 3 Scene 2 the two of them developed a kind of anarchic complicity.

It was in this context that the actors embarked on Act 4 of the play, where for the first time, away from Padua, we began to see the actor playing Petruchio as an abuser rather than a clown. What transpired in this act was that Petruchio was able to distort and abuse the relationship which the two of them had set up earlier in the play, so that rather than openly victimising her, he could treat her as if she had broken some intimate agreement and betrayed him. She, on the other hand found herself appealing to him not as a stranger but as someone she had felt to be a kindred spirit, and in whom she had placed a certain trust, which meant that, even in the most abusive scenes, the two actors continued to have a bizarre dependency on one another.

The result of this was that the actors began to find a much deeper truth and logic in the characters and their relationships than if they had merely tried to play stereotyped versions of patriarch and feminist throughout the play. In the distorted world of Petruchio's house, they made an extraordinary actor's discovery first-hand – that role-play, if it goes on for long enough, becomes more real than the reality it replaces.

As they worked through Act 4, the actors began to add more layers to their relationship. By continuing with his 'taming' long after it had ceased to be necessary, and by allowing himself to see opposition and rebellion where none existed, in the servants and tradespeople as well as in Katherine herself, Petruchio began to appear rather mentally unbalanced, and his tantrums seemed to be more about his problems than hers. It was almost as if his absolute permission to abuse her was driving him slightly insane, while she came to seem more and more like someone humouring and placating a mentally ill husband.

The rest of the company, who were observing, noted that Katherine was no longer submitting to Petruchio, but to the absoluteness of male power in her society, which had affected him like an illness. In other words, what these actors discovered from the text was that the patriarchal society had so skewed the balance of power in their relationship that these two otherwise well-matched young people were forced into a strange and distorted struggle, and finally into a tense and uneasy equilibrium. The actor playing Katherine ceased to be concerned with her feminist beliefs, or the rights and wrongs of the case, and realised that her only hope of gaining even the most basic social and domestic influence was to embrace an absolute obedience to Petruchio's will. Ironically, by learning to placate him at every point, she was able to curb the excesses of his power and to temper his more abusive outbursts, and thereby could enable both to survive in the marriage.

Katherine's famous final monologue about a woman's duty to her husband, which the actor had previously been unable to deliver without irony, could now be delivered with absolute truth, not because the company wished the audience to take away a pro-patriarchal reading of the play, but because they wanted to show how, for the sake of her survival and sanity, Katherine had been forced to acknowledge her own helplessness in the face of the patriarchy, unlike the other women who fooled themselves into believing they could control their men within the system. By submitting to the inevitable and deciding to buy into the patriarchal system, the actor playing Katherine gave the clearest indication possible to the women in the play (and to those in the audience) of how precarious their power actually was, and how easily it could be snatched away from them. This might be seen as a gloomy and pessimistic reading of the piece; it might also be regarded as extremely radical, urging women not to settle for the illusion of power while allowing the system to remain fundamentally unchanged.

Without imposing anything on the text the actors had discovered and realised its political potency, simply through their search for something that made sense both to the text and to themselves. They achieved this by being true to themselves as actors, making all their discoveries within the space, and making the text the basis for everything they did, even within their physical improvisations.

Afterwards these actors realised that what they had found in rehearsal was far more complex than anything they could have dreamed up just by reading the play, but they were also intrigued to discover that both the play and the characters as written made much more sense to them than when they started out, simply because they had trusted the text and made it work for them rather than searching for solutions outside of it. It was probably only in retrospect that the actors really had a sense of who their characters were, but this didn't matter – it only meant that the characters continued to grow, change and develop even to the last performance.

One of the things you can learn from this is that you do not have to impose realist notions of 'character' on Shakespeare. By understanding how the language works and responding truthfully to what you find in the space you can make the play not just make sense but make sense *for you*. The same is true to some extent with all plays, but the beauty of Shakespeare is that the text alone supplies you with almost everything you need to unlock the play. Other forms of text give fewer clues, guide you less, demand more from you to make them work, but it is still the simple chemistry of 'you, the text and the space' which you should start with, whatever techniques you may have at your fingertips for opening up the text within the space.

If you are the sort of actor who has to 'know' your character like some sort of biographer before you step into the space, or have already decided how your character feels about the other characters before they start, you will be so weighed down with your knowledge that when the chemistry starts to happen you will be unable to respond to it. It is worth reminding ourselves that Shakespeare did not write for such actors. Nor did he write for actors who impose interpretations or steer their scenes along preordained paths, either because they don't trust the text or because they want to appear inventive and bold. Having said that, if you can allow yourself to discover Shakespeare as if for the first time, rather than as something to be dutifully played according to some convention, you will free yourself from the debilitating notion that the job of an actor is to give people what they already know and expect to see. With Shakespeare more than any other playwright you must pursue the subtle chemistry between the text and the living person, and if you can be open and courageous enough to let that chemistry occur, then what you offer will be truly unique.

Working with Shakespeare's text should be the ultimate in empowerment for you, whether or not you ever perform it professionally. So much has been written about these plays, so much debate has gone on about what they mean and how they should be played, and yet you, the actor, have the right to pick them up and make them yours, possibly even to find in them things which no-one has seen before. If you can achieve this with the most revered and studied of playwrights, you will have discovered the basic art of the actor – to give the text life and make it resonate using your own life and the rhythms of your own body.

17

Concluding Thoughts

I have been attempting to achieve two things in this book. One is to show how acting techniques and acting styles are not absolutes, but are the product of the society from which they emerge, fulfilling artistic and social functions specific to a particular time and place. The second aim has been to provide an alternative set of practical approaches to actor training, placing emphasis on social interaction and social transaction rather than on the inner life of the individual, and offering you practical techniques for keeping the text alive in the space.

Having used these techniques for some years, I know they work, and that they produce actors who are outwardly focused, open and generous to one another. Transactional Improvisation helps actors to understand their interactions with others and to break out of habitual patterns, while the Meisner-based repetition work trains them to respond to each other without self-censorship. Those who have accepted and taken on board this training see the ensemble and the company as the key to success, and are used to negotiating everything in the space rather than in their own heads.

What surprises many actors once they have done their groundwork vocally, physically and intellectually, is that the work in the space can become self-energising and enjoyable rather than grindingly, drainingly exhausting. Ironically, sometimes actors assume they are 'doing it wrong' because they haven't found their work painful. Others worry that the external appearance of their acting is at odds with what they at first imagined it would be, and that it therefore can't be right. They measure themselves against other actors' performances which have at some point appeared to them delightful, moving or thrilling, and they assume that to succeed as actors they must become like the actors of the past.

It is important therefore that as you begin your training you should be able to place what has gone before in its proper context, understanding that all acting styles are merely sign systems, and that performances are there to be understood rather than admired. There is no definitive 'right' way to act; the choices which you make about both *what* is communicated and *how* it is communicated, depend largely on how you read and understand the text and what in the text you find most important. This being the case, even if much of what you do in the moment is visceral and instinctual, you need to be aware, before and after, of what you have chosen to communicate, and what, in so doing, you have chosen *not* to communicate.

In the twentieth century, the age of Stanislavski and Lee Strasberg, most actors in Britain and America would have considered psychological realism to be paramount in their work. With the advent of psychoanalysis the western world began to understand human actions less through simplistic notions of good and evil and more in terms of complex mental and emotional processes. The dark and unpredictable depths of the unconscious mind became an object of fascination, and our attempts to represent the complexity of human psychology came to be synonymous with the actor's art. The neurosis and emotional damage which we were recognising in ourselves through psychoanalysis became both deified and demonised in our actors, until we became utterly absorbed and fascinated by the notion of the damaged and alienated individual. Actors both onstage and in movies reflected our own angst and emotions back at us in a glamourised and heightened form, making us feel validated, acceptable, and less alone. We loved, admired and worshipped them for what they gave us.

This in itself may not have been a bad thing. Drama which offers us our own humanity in all its manifestations can be a purging and healing force, arousing compassion, understanding and a sense of belonging. The problem with focusing on the emotional and psychological state of the individual, however, is that this can draw attention away from the social gestures and transactions which continually reinforce and influence that individual's behaviour, and which may present a different interpretation of the text. Drama, as we have seen, is a distillation of life, and you can choose through your performance to foreground or background different features of a situation, drawing attention to one aspect and away from another, often without the audience even realising that these choices have been made on their behalf. For this reason you have an awesome responsibility to question and analyse the choices you make.

This book is not seeking to mould anyone into a particular sort of actor, nor to insist that acting should be seen in a particular way. However, my final piece of advice to all those setting out to be actors is this: Remember that drama has the power to reveal and liberate, but also the power to conceal and indoctrinate. Above all it has an artistic and social duty to shine the spotlight onto our social interactions and to show us where we could have done things differently. As such drama is a potent political tool, and never more than in the twenty-first century, when a larger proportion of the population than ever before has access to it. While claiming to reflect our lives as they really are, film and television drama can in fact be feeding our fear, our hopelessness, our grief and our blind dependency, while concealing the ways in which we could perhaps choose differently, reinvent both ourselves and our society and make positive changes to our lives and communities.

While the actor is himself not solely responsible for creating drama, the actor does have responsibility for interpreting the text, and in the modern world this is not just an artistic but a social responsibility. If the actor's only interest is in signing to the audience the depth of his own emotional struggles, then that is all the audience will see. They may feel moved, they may be impressed, but they will not be empowered. Such drama places a sticking plaster on our ills – it does not offer a diagnosis or a cure.

I would like to send actors out into the industry who understand their art in its fullest sense, and who, despite the hardships, competition and cynicism within the profession, never lose sight of the most basic function of drama, which is to shine a light on this confused and troubled world, and to use their art to try and make sense of it.

Bibliography

SOURCES

Bate, J, *The Genius of Shakespeare*, OUP 1998
Chekhov, M, *On the Technique of Acting*, Harper Perennial
    1991
Counsell, C, *Signs of Performance*, Routledge 1996
Hodge, A, *Twentieth Century Actor Training*, Routledge 1999
Longwell, D, *Sanford Meisner on Acting*, Vintage 1987
Mamet, D, *True and False*, Faber & Faber 1998
Silverberg, L, *The Sanford Meisner Approach* (Workbooks
    I & II) Smith & Kraus 1997
Stanislavski, C, *An Actor Prepares*, (Trans: Hapgood, E)
    Methuen 1980
—— *Building a Character*, (Trans: Hapgood, E) Methuen 1979
—— *My Life in Art*, (Trans: Robbins, J) Methuen 1980

SUGGESTED FURTHER READING

Brook, P, *Evoking (and Forgetting) Shakespeare*, Nick Hern
    Books 2003
Berry, C, *The Actor and the Text*, Virgin 1996
Callery, D, *Through the Body*, Nick Hern Books 2002
Houseman, B, *Finding Your Voice*, Nick Hern Books 2002
Linklater, K, *Freeing the Natural Voice*, Drama Publishers
    1976
Marshall, L, *The Body Speaks*, Methuen 2001
Rodenburg, P, *The Right to Speak*, Methuen 1992

Endnotes

1 Counsell, C, *Signs of Performance*, Routledge 1996
2 Mamet, *True and False*, Faber and Faber 1998
3 *Ibid.* p 9
4 *Ibid.* p 20
5 *Ibid.* p 58
6 *Ibid.* p 71
7 A David Mamet play about the competitive world of real-estate agents, first performed in 1984 on Broadway
8 Action verbs are a modification of Stanislavski's techniques for breaking down text. Uta Hagen in particular describes this technique in *Respect for Acting* (Macmillan USA 1973). See also Chapter 8 of this book
9 The eponymous character from the play of that name by Henrik Ibsen, first performed in 1890
10 Barba, E , & Savarese, N, *A Dictionary of Theatre Anthropology*, Routledge 1991
11 Author of *True and False (op. cit.)*, a book which challenges the need for text breakdown and other elements of actor training.
12 Linklater, K, *Freeing the Natural Voice*, Drama Books 1976
13 Houseman, B, *Finding Your Voice*, Nick Hern Books 2002
14 Rodenburg, P, *The Right to Speak*, Methuen 1992
15 Berry, C, *The Actor and the Text*, Virgin 1996
16 Formerly a PG Dip, this course has in recent years gained MA status

17 The term 'given circumstances' was coined by Stanislavski, and originally meant the *character's* circumstances within the play world and the situation. The
Meisner definition includes both the *character's* and the
actor's circumstances, including the text itself, the set
moves, and the theatrical space. See **Trust and Acceptance** in Chapter 3 of this book
18 Quotation from a second-year actor's working notebook
for a production of *Oliver Twist*, 2004
19 Mamet, D, *op. cit.*
20 From *Richard III*, Act 1 Scene 3
21 From *Richard III*, Act 1 Scene 2
22 From *Twelfth Night*, Act 1 Scene 1
23 From *Twelfth Night*, Act 3 Scene 1